COMPACT *Research*

Video
Games

Current Issues

ReferencePoint
Press™

San Diego, CA

Other books in the Compact Research series include:

Drugs
Alcohol
Club Drugs
Cocaine and Crack
Hallucinogens
Heroin
Inhalants
Marijuana
Methamphetamine
Nicotine and Tobacco
Performance-Enhancing Drugs

Current Issues
Biomedical Ethics
The Death Penalty
Energy Alternatives
Free Speech
Global Warming and Climate Change
Gun Control
Illegal Immigration
National Security
Nuclear Weapons and Security
Obesity
Terrorist Attacks
World Energy Crisis

Diseases and Disorders
Anorexia
Hepatitis
Meningitis
Phobias
STDs

Video Games

by Peggy J. Parks

Current Issues

ReferencePoint
Press™

San Diego, CA

For more information, contact:
ReferencePoint Press, Inc.
PO Box 27779
San Diego, CA 92198
www.ReferencePointPress.com

Picture credits:
Maury Aaseng: 33–35, 48–50, 65–67, 81–84
AP Images: 15, 16

LIBRARY OF CONGRESS CATALOGING-IN-PUBLICATION DATA

Parks, Peggy J., 1951–
    Video games / by Peggy J. Parks.
        p. cm. — (Compact research series)
    Includes bibliographical references and index.
    ISBN-13: 978-1-60152-053-1 (hardback)
    ISBN-10: 1-60152-053-0 (hardback)
    1. Video games—Social aspects—Juvenile literature. 2. Video games—Psychological aspects—Juvenile literature. I. Title.
    GV1469.34.S52P37 2008
    794.8'1019—dc22
                                                                2007049886

Contents

Foreword   6

Video Games at a Glance   8

Overview   10

Are Video Games Harmful?   21
     Primary Source Quotes   28
     Facts and Illustrations   32

Do Video Games Cause Violent Crime?   36
     Primary Source Quotes   43
     Facts and Illustrations   47

How Do Video Games Affect Mental and
     Physical Health?   51
     Primary Source Quotes   60
     Facts and Illustrations   64

Should Video Games Be Regulated?   68
     Primary Source Quotes   76
     Facts and Illustrations   80

Key People and Advocacy Groups   86

Chronology   88

Related Organizations   90

For Further Research   94

Source Notes   97

List of Illustrations   100

Index   101

About the Author   104

Foreword

“ **Where is the knowledge we have lost in information?** ”

—"The Rock," T.S. Eliot.

As modern civilization continues to evolve, its ability to create, store, distribute, and access information expands exponentially. The explosion of information from all media continues to increase at a phenomenal rate. By 2020 some experts predict the worldwide information base will double every 73 days. While access to diverse sources of information and perspectives is paramount to any democratic society, information alone cannot help people gain knowledge and understanding. Information must be organized and presented clearly and succinctly in order to be understood. The challenge in the digital age becomes not the creation of information, but how best to sort, organize, enhance, and present information.

ReferencePoint Press developed the *Compact Research* series with this challenge of the information age in mind. More than any other subject area today, researching current issues can yield vast, diverse, and unqualified information that can be intimidating and overwhelming for even the most advanced and motivated researcher. The *Compact Research* series offers a compact, relevant, intelligent, and conveniently organized collection of information covering a variety of current topics ranging from illegal immigration and methamphetamine to diseases such as anorexia and meningitis.

The series focuses on three types of information: objective single-author narratives, opinion-based primary source quotations, and facts and statistics. The clearly written objective narratives provide context and reliable background information. Primary source quotes are carefully selected and cited, exposing the reader to differing points of view. And facts and statistics sections aid the reader in evaluating perspectives. Presenting these key types of information creates a richer, more balanced learning experience.

For better understanding and convenience, the series enhances information by organizing it into narrower topics and adding design features that make it easy for a reader to identify desired content. For example, in *Compact Research: Illegal Immigration*, a chapter covering the economic impact of illegal immigration has an objective narrative explaining the various ways the economy is impacted, a balanced section of numerous primary source quotes on the topic, followed by facts and full-color illustrations to encourage evaluation of contrasting perspectives.

The ancient Roman philosopher Lucius Annaeus Seneca wrote, "It is quality rather than quantity that matters." More than just a collection of content, the *Compact Research* series is simply committed to creating, finding, organizing, and presenting the most relevant and appropriate amount of information on a current topic in a user-friendly style that invites, intrigues, and fosters understanding.

Video Games at a Glance

Popularity

In 2006 worldwide spending on video games was more than $31 billion. In the United States more than $7.4 billion was spent on video games in 2006—almost triple the sales of 1996.

Regulation and Control

Although some countries have laws that govern the sale and/or rental of video games, the United States has no such laws. The video game industry monitors its own activities.

Game Ratings

The Entertainment Software Rating Board (ESRB) is responsible for rating video games. Seven different rating symbols may be printed on the front of game boxes: Early Childhood (EC); Everyone (E); Players 10 and older (E10+); Teen (T); Mature (M); and Adults Only (AO). The ESRB also furnishes descriptions of potentially offensive or sensitive content. These ratings and content descriptors are only meant to be parental advisories.

Connection with Violent Crime

Some people argue that school shootings and other acts of violence can be traced to the criminals' fondness for playing violent video games and then acting them out in real life.

Video Game Addiction

Although it is a controversial issue, psychotherapists have treated many people who show signs of addiction to video games.

Health Effects

Excessive video game play has been linked to a number of physical problems such as back pain, bad posture, eye strain, headaches, and tendonitis, which is often called Nintendo thumb, joystick thumb, or Nintenditis. An even more serious threat is deep vein thrombosis (DVT), or blood clots, which can be life threatening.

Failed Legislation

A number of states have attempted to pass legislation that would make it illegal for retailers to sell or rent M- or AO-rated videos to minors. Citing violations of First Amendment rights, federal judges have struck all of these proposed laws down.

Overview

> **The messages for most of these games, especially the ones young boys are playing, are: violence is fun; violence is entertaining; no one really gets hurt, and if they get hurt, it's funny, or it doesn't hurt them. When you spend hours playing these games, you are getting those kinds of ideas in your head, as opposed to ideas of empathy, compassion, values of helping people, or doing anything socially constructive.**
>
> —Daphne White, quoted in *Religion & Ethics*.

> **Computer and video games are an increasingly powerful medium, providing engaging ways for people to learn, be entertained, and connect and communicate with each other.**
>
> —Robert Wood Johnson Foundation, "$8.25-Million Research Program to Investigate Design Strategies and Benefits of Interactive Games to Improve Health and Health Care."

In the spring of 1962 a team of graduate students from the Massachusetts Institute of Technology (MIT) were putting the finishing touches on a computer game called *Spacewar*. The game's developer, a programmer named Steve "Slug" Russell, had created it to demonstrate the capabilities of MIT's new computer. *Spacewar* was designed for two players, who used toggle switches to fire virtual missiles at each other from their own spaceships. A player's goal was to hit and destroy the enemy, while at the same time avoiding the gravitational pull of the sun. Steven

L. Kent describes this in his book, *The Ultimate History of Video Games*: "The best players learned how to accelerate into the sun's gravitational field, loop around, and catch slower opponents off guard. Hovering too close or flying into the sun meant death."[1] Russell finished perfecting *Spacewar* and then made it available free of charge to computer laboratories so other programmers could play it. He had developed the world's first interactive computer game—yet he had no way of knowing that his creation would spark the beginning of an entertainment revolution.

> " As video games have continued to evolve and grow more sophisticated, their popularity has skyrocketed—and controversy over them has grown as well. "

Today's video games are so animated, so colorful, and so highly realistic, it is hard to imagine that their distant relative was such a simple, basic game. As video games have continued to evolve and grow more sophisticated, their popularity has skyrocketed—and controversy over them has grown as well. Unlike *Spacewar*, in which missiles were depicted by mere points of light, ultraviolent games such as *Grand Theft Auto: San Andreas*, *Carmageddon*, and *Manhunt* allow players to injure, maim, and kill in eerily realistic ways. Some people are convinced that players, especially younger children and teenagers, can be influenced in negative ways, even provoked to aggressive behavior and violence, by these types of games. Others argue that video games are no more harmful to players than television, movies, and books.

The Growing Popularity of Video Games

According to the Entertainment Software Association (ESA), 69 percent of American heads of households play games on a personal computer, game console, or portable game player. The average age of people who play video games (called gamers) is about 30, although 31 percent are under the age of 18. The National Institute on Media and the Family reports that nearly half of all "heavy gamers" are in the age range of 6 to 17 years old. In 2006 worldwide spending on video games was more than

$31 billion. More than $7.4 billion was spent on video and computer games in the United States—almost triple the sales of 1996.

How Are Video Games Regulated?

Countries such as Germany, Australia, New Zealand, Ireland, China, and Brazil, have laws in place that ban certain video games, but no such laws exist in the United States. Some people support legislation that would regulate the sale or rental of video games. To date, none of these proponents of video game legislation has been successful.

The video game industry is self-regulated, meaning it controls and monitors its own activities. In 1994 the Entertainment Software Rating Board was created as a regulatory body responsible for applying and enforcing video game ratings and advertising. Today the ESRB uses seven different rating symbols that are printed on the front of the game box. These ratings are: Early Childhood (EC); Everyone (E); players 10 and older (E10+); Teen (T); Mature (M); and Adults Only (AO). The ESRB also furnishes descriptions of potentially offensive or sensitive content, such as "Blood and Gore," "Mature Humor," "Strong Language," "Sexual Content," and "Partial Nudity," which are printed on the back of the game boxes. These ratings, however, are only meant to be parental advisories. No laws regulate the sale or rental of video games, although many retailers enforce their own policies to keep mature video games out of the hands of children.

Do Video Games Influence the Choices Kids Make?

One major element in the video game debate is what role they play in the choices young people make. Will Wright, the designer of the popular game *The Sims 2*, says that playing video games can be a valuable tool in teaching kids to tell right from wrong. Unlike movies, which are a passive activity, players are in control of video games, and they are responsible for what happens to fictional characters. If they consciously bring harm to the characters, they are likely to feel guilty about it. Henry Jenkins, a professor at MIT, agrees with Wright's viewpoint, saying that video games can help teach kids how to make good choices: "Many current games are designed to be ethical testing grounds. They allow players to navigate an expansive and open-ended world, make their own choices and witness their consequences. . . . In the right circumstances, we can be encouraged to examine our own values by seeing how we behave within virtual space."[2]

Video Games and Children

Even when video games are M-rated, research has shown that teenagers and children often play them. In a March 2005 survey by the Kaiser Family Foundation, only about 20 percent of kids reported that their parents had any rules for video game use. Australian writer Christopher Bantick says that his 11-year-old son was in a store and watched a father buy the violent computer game *Manhunt* for his son, who was of similar age. Bantick explains: "The game, banned in New Zealand for its extreme violent content, is rated MA 15+ in Australia. There is no higher classification here. My son was shocked at the knowing smile between the father and the son as he passed the game to him. Is this responsible parenting? Hardly."[3]

According to James Paul Gee, a professor at the University of Wisconsin, most parents are unaware of what their kids are doing on the computer or the video game machine. Gee believes, though, that video games are good for children because they teach thinking and problem-solving skills, as well as develop creativity. He says that kids should start playing games such as *Dr. Seuss's Cat in the Hat, Winnie the Pooh, Pajama Sam*, and *Spy Fox* when they are as young as three years old.

People who are concerned about the negative effects of video games say the biggest risk is to young children because they are impressionable, easily frightened, and have difficulty distinguishing reality from fantasy. Also, the violence that is featured in video games is often there to add flair and humor. This can be confusing for young children, who are just starting to learn about values and whether certain behaviors are right or wrong. Another factor is the marketing of products that are spawned from video games. Even if

> " Countries such as Germany, Australia, New Zealand, Ireland, China, and Brazil, have laws in place that ban certain video games, but no such laws exist in the United States. "

young children are not exposed to video games designed for older players, they may be exposed to toys based on the characters. For example, the Media Awareness Network says that the violent, point-and-shoot video game *Duke Nukem* is rated for players who are 17 and older, but it "spawned action figures that were marketed to children under 8 years old."[4] The *Halo 3* series is M-rated, with content descriptors "Blood and Gore" and "Violence," yet action figures are sold on Amazon.com for ages 10 and up. The video game *God of War* is M-rated with content descriptors "Blood and Gore, Intense Violence, Nudity, Sexual Themes, and Strong Language," yet action figures from the game are recommended for ages eight years and up. All video games in the violent series *Mortal Kombat* are rated M, but action figures based on the game are advertised on Amazon.com for children above three years old.

Video Games and Violent Crime

No issue is more hotly debated than whether violent video games can spawn real-life violence. After the April 2007 massacre of 32 students at Virginia Tech University, Florida attorney Jack Thompson lashed out at the developers of *Counter-Strike*, a video game that real-life shooter Cho Seung-Hui had reportedly played often. "This is not rocket science," Thompson says. "When a kid who has never killed anyone in his life goes on a rampage and looks like the Terminator, he's a video gamer."[5]

> Gamers become more perceptive by training their brains to analyze things quickly, they hone skills in problem solving and decision making, and they develop better concentration.

Many others, however, believe it is ludicrous to blame video games for crimes committed in real life. The position of the ESA is that video games are no more responsible for violent crimes than movies, books, and music. In their article, "Target Real Violence, Not Video Games," Robert D. Richards and Clay Calvert say that no one has ever proven through independent research that video games are harmful to children or that they actually lead to violent behavior. "Hundreds of thousands of kids who

After the April 2007 massacre of 32 students at Virginia Tech University, Florida attorney Jack Thompson lashed out at the developers of Counter-Strike, *a video game that real-life shooter Cho Seung-Hui had reportedly played often. Here, law enforcement officers are seen helping a wounded student during the Virginia Tech shooting.*

play video games, the vast majority of which do not portray violence, will never assault, attack, or otherwise harm anyone."[6]

Do Video Games Make Kids Smarter?

In July 2007 researchers at the University of Michigan and the University of Texas performed a video game study with data based on the diaries of nearly 1,500 kids from aged 10 to 19. Those who said they regularly played video games spent 30 percent less time reading and 34 percent less time doing homework than nongamers. Separate studies by the National Institute on Media and the Family found that the amount of time kids spent playing video games was related to poorer grades in school and attention problems.

Some video games require physical action, such as Nintendo's Wii Fit (above), which incorporates physical movements into a game. There are also video games that are designed to motivate kids to become healthier by eating right and exercising. The National Institutes of Health is funding the development of several science-fiction video games that focus on health.

Other research has resulted in quite different findings, indicating that video games can actually enhance kids' intelligence. Gamers become more perceptive by training their brains to analyze things quickly, they hone skills in problem solving and decision making, and they develop better concentration. Gee explains how kids benefit intellectually from playing video games: "They have to discover the rules of the game and how to think strategically. Like any problem solving that is good for your head, it makes you smarter."[7] Gee also says that video games can expand kids' interest in different kinds of topics. He cites *Age of Mythology*, a strategic game designed for teens that involves characters leading armies into battle. He has seen children who play the game become so fascinated with mythology that they want to read books about it, do online research about it, and draw pictures about mythological characters.

Video Games and Health

One concern that is often raised about video games is that many kids spend too much time playing them. Studies show that children who spend most of their time playing video games are not physically active, are often heavier, and are more likely to be overweight or even obese. Yet not all video games are sedentary entertainment. Some require physical action, such as Nintendo's Wii *Boxing*, which incorporates physical movements into game play using motion-sensitive wireless controllers. Holding a controller in each hand, players throw punches into the air to control the on-screen action.

There are also video games that are designed to motivate kids to become healthier by eating right and exercising. The National Institutes of Health (NIH) is funding the development of several science-fiction video games that focus on health. In one of them, called *Nanoswarm: Invasion from Inner Space*, the characters are four teenagers who travel through the human body in a tiny ship in a quest to defeat microscopic robots that cause obesity and disease. In another game, called *Escape from Diab*, the main character must help other kids overcome Etes, the evil king who prevents all his subjects from exercising and eating healthy meals.

Are Video Games Addictive?

In the 1940s Irish author and scholar C.S. Lewis described addiction as an "ever-increasing craving for an ever-diminishing pleasure."[8] People can become physically addicted to substances such as alcohol, drugs, cigarettes, or caffeine, or psychologically addicted to behaviors like compulsive gambling, spending, overeating, or sex. Some researchers are convinced that video games can be equally as addictive.

According to the National Institute on Media and the Family, the symptoms of video game addiction are much like symptoms of other addictions, including obsessive and deceitful behavior, neglecting responsibilities, and alienation from other people. The organization says that video game addiction is an alarming health issue: "Some of the most popular online community games practically demand an obsessive and time-consuming approach to play. As with any addiction, once children are hooked, it is very difficult for them to quit."[9]

> No issue is more hotly debated than whether violent video games can spawn real-life violence.

People who reject the idea of video game addiction say that the games are no more addictive than any other hobby. In 2007 the American Medical Association began debating whether to formally classify excessive video game playing as an addiction. Stuart Gitlow, a psychiatrist affiliated with the American Society of Addiction Medicine, disapproves of such a move. He says that while excessive game playing may be a problem for some people, it is not a medical problem and should not be considered an addiction. He explains: "If you are not putting time into hobbies and interests, [life] would be pretty boring. If it wasn't an addiction with baseball, model trains and cars, then it isn't with video games."[10]

How Do Video Games Affect Social Skills?

Some people believe that kids who spend much of their time playing video games become socially isolated and purposely avoid spending time with family and friends. According to the National Institute on Media and the Family, the reason for this is because so many of the games are played alone. When kids are content to spend hours and hours glued to a computer monitor, they are less likely to seek the companionship of other people.

Not all video games are limited to solitary play, though. Many games are specifically designed for multiple players. Parents, for instance, often play games with their children. According to the ESA, 80 percent of gamer parents surveyed in 2005 said they played video games with their children, and 66 percent said that playing games had brought their families closer together. Findings of a June 2007 study by researchers at Massachusetts General Hospital's Center for Mental Health and

Media showed that video game play enhanced socialization, rather than detracted from it. Cheryl K. Olson, lead author of the study, explains: "Contrary to the stereotype of the solitary gamer with no social skills, we found that children who play M-rated games are actually more likely to play in groups—in the same room, or over the Internet. Boys' friendships in particular often center around video games."[11]

Video Games and Negative Stereotypes

Much of the controversy over video games is around the issue of violence. But another issue causes concern for many people: that the games reinforce negative stereotypes. Larry Fitcheard is a black game enthusiast from Texas who says that video games are slanted toward making white people look more favorable than blacks. He explains: "Especially in some of the earlier games, you couldn't pick a black character—it gave the impression that black people didn't exist." Although Fitcheard adds that black characters eventually were featured in some games, this was not necessarily positive. "The bad guy would be the black guy, the criminal needing to be arrested would be the black guy, and the hero would be the white guy. If the black guy is always the thief, then after a while you start to think that's how you should be, or you think that's how black people are."[12]

Whether video games reinforce sexual stereotypes is another issue of concern for many people. Most games feature male characters, and females are often portrayed as helpless victims; sexually provocative vamps with voluptuous, perfect bodies; or prostitutes. Freelance writer and video game enthusiast Aleah Tierney explains her views on this: "As a

> " Whether video games reinforce sexual stereotypes is another issue of concern for many people. "

female gamer, I'm a stranger in a strange land. I play in a male-created virtual space. Male video game characters embody the fantasy of what men want to be. Female characters represent the fantasy women men want. But I have my own desires, and most games fall far short of fulfilling them."[13] More and more women are becoming video game fans like Tierney, and as a result, female roles in the games are starting to change. Increasing numbers of games feature strong, powerful female characters. One example is the video game *Super Metroid*, whose heroine is the female superhero, Samus Aran.

Video Games in the Future

Video games will continue growing even more popular in the coming years. The consulting firm PriceWaterhouseCoopers predicts that world-wide video game sales will reach close to $50 billion by 2011, with the greatest amount of growth in online and wireless games. Designers say that in the future, video games will be far more sophisticated, graphic, and realistic than they are today. Douglas Lowenstein, former president of the ESA, offers his perspective: "The video game industry is entering a new era, an era where technology and creativity will fuse to produce some of the most stunning entertainment of the 21st Century. Decades from now, cultural historians will look back at this time and say it is when the definition of entertainment changed forever."[14]

Are Video Games Harmful?

> 66 There really isn't any room for doubt. Aggressive game playing leads to aggressive behavior. The naysayers don't have a leg to stand on. 99
>
> —Craig Anderson, quoted in Bob Condor, "Living Well: Violent Video Games Just Can't Be Good for Kids."

> 66 The evidence does not establish that video games, because of their interactive nature or otherwise, are any more harmful than violent television, movies, Internet sites or other speech-related exposures. 99
>
> —United States District Judge Ronald Whyte, quoted in Jeff Taylor, "He'll Be Back."

Whether video games are harmful is a controversial issue, as well as a highly subjective one. Most game enthusiasts reject the notion that games can cause harm, calling it an unfair generalization with no basis in fact. But even though these games are obviously not harmful in the same way that playing with guns, knives, or explosives can be, many people insist that the games can and do cause harm, especially to children and teenagers. They argue that heavy game players become desensitized to aggression and violence, and that video game play steals time away from other activities such as reading, playing outside, or doing homework. Another argument is that kids become so immersed in video game play that they find it difficult to break away and even get angry when asked to put down the game controls and do something else. Christopher Bantick offers an example: "Any parent who has had to ask a child to come away from a computer during a games session is likely to have an angry response. Why? Deprived of their regular fix, children can demonstrate the symptoms of addiction. Going cold turkey is not pretty. A similar response isn't usually forthcoming if a child is asked to stop reading—or playing with Legos for that matter."[15]

Did Video Game Addiction Lead to Suicide?

Shawn Woolley's favorite pastime was playing *EverQuest*, a never-ending online fantasy game that attracts hundreds of thousands of game enthusiasts all over the world. Players operate in a three-dimensional virtual world, and they control their characters through quests, or missions, that involve slaying monsters and gathering treasures. The more successful they are in their quests, the stronger and more powerful they become. Woolley, a shy, overweight 21-year-old man from Wisconsin, started playing *EverQuest* in 2000, and according to his mother, Liz Woolley, within a year the game had taken over his life. He quit his job, cut off all contact with his family, refused to answer the door when people knocked, and spent nearly every waking moment in front of the computer playing *EverQuest*.

> Whether video games are harmful is a controversial issue, as well as a highly subjective one.

On Thanksgiving morning in 2001, Liz Woolley went to her son's apartment. For two days prior to that she had gone there and pounded on his doors and windows but got no response. Finally, she became frightened and broke in by cutting through the chain lock on his door. She saw dirty clothes, dozens of empty pizza boxes, fast-food wrappers scattered everywhere—and she also saw Shawn, slumped over in a chair in front of his computer. He had shot himself to death with a .22-caliber rifle; the gun was lying beside him on the floor, and *EverQuest* was still on the glowing computer screen. Distraught over her son's death, Liz Woolley blamed Sony Online Entertainment, the creator of the game, for his suicide. She acknowledges that he suffered from depression and other problems, but she is convinced that Sony deliberately added features to *EverQuest* to keep players online for hours at a time. "It's like any other addiction," she says. "Either you die, go insane or you quit. My son died."[16]

Jay Parker, a chemical dependency counselor from Redmond, Washington, says that because Shawn had a poor self-image and was isolated, depressed, and lonely, he was the type of person who is most susceptible to video game addiction. Parker adds, though, that Shawn's tragic death involved a number of factors that were not necessarily related to video games. Parker and David Walsh, the president of the National Institute on Media and the Family, share the viewpoint that video games are not inherently bad. They both say that becoming seriously addicted, especially to the point of being suicidal, is not at all typical behavior for the average video game enthusiast.

> " Distraught over her son's death, Liz Woolley blamed Sony Online Entertainment, the creator of the game, for his suicide. "

In the late 1990s researchers from Hammersmith Hospital in London studied video game addiction. They were looking for connections between video game play and the brain's levels of dopamine, a chemical that is released by the brain when someone engages in pleasurable activities such as sex or enjoying a good meal, or ingests certain types of drugs such as narcotics, nicotine, or caffeine. When subjects played video games, dopamine levels in their brains doubled. The researchers concluded that a physical addiction to video games is indeed a possibility.

How Video Games Affect Behavior

Although it is hotly debated whether there is a connection between video game play and aggressive behavior, some researchers insist that there is. In 2005 psychologists Sonya S. Brady and Karen A. Matthews conducted a laboratory study at a university campus that involved 100 young men from 18 to 21 years old. The participants were randomly assigned to play one of 2 video games: *The Simpsons: Hit and Run*, considered low-violence;

or *Grand Theft Auto III*, considered high-violence. Brady and Matthews found distinct differences between the two groups. In comparison to the men who played *The Simpsons* game, those who played *Grand Theft Auto III* showed elevated blood pressure; negative emotions, hostility, and uncooperative behavior; and more permissive attitudes toward violence, alcohol use, and use of drugs. The findings of the study were published in the April 2006 issue of *Archives of Pediatrics & Adolescent Medicine*, in which the authors wrote: "Media violence exposure may play a role in the development of negative attitudes and behaviors related to health. Although youth growing up in violent homes and communities may become more physiologically aroused by media violence exposure, all youth appear to be at risk for potentially negative outcomes."[17]

Henry Jenkins believes that studies showing a link between video games and aggressive behavior or violence are the product of researchers who represent a relatively narrow type of research known as "media effects." Jenkins says such studies use flawed methodologies and result in findings that are inconclusive. He explains:

> The laboratory context is radically different from the environments where games would normally be played. Most studies found a correlation, not a causal relationship, which means the research could simply show that aggressive people like aggressive entertainment. . . . If there is a consensus emerging around this research, it is that violent video games may be one risk factor—when coupled with other more immediate, real-world influences—which can contribute to antisocial behavior. [18]

"This Wasn't the Game's Fault"

After a fiery car crash in Toronto, Canada, in January 2006, media reports speculated that a video game might be partly to blame. Two teenager drivers were involved in a street race and were traveling about 90 miles per hour (145kph) in a 30-mile-per hour (48kph) zone. One of the speeding cars, a Mercedes-Benz, slammed into a taxicab that was making a left turn, and the taxi driver was killed instantly. Police officers investigating the crash found a copy of the racing video game *Need for Speed* on the front seat of the Mercedes, which led some people to conclude that the driver's reckless actions might have been inspired by the game. Police detective Paul Lobsinger says that as tragic as the accident was, the video game was not responsible: "There is a small percentage who have difficulty separating reality and simulation, or fantasy. This wasn't the game's fault. There are millions who play this game and don't go out and do this."[19]

"A Balanced Entertainment Diet"

Many people insist that kids can gain tremendous benefits from playing video games. The key, they say, is to use common sense—any entertainment can potentially be unhealthy if it is excessive. Richard Gallagher, a psychologist and director of the Parenting Institute at the NYU Child Study Center, explains:

> Used in moderation, the advantages can be very helpful. The negative effects are found with excessive play, so the benefits may outweigh any possible negative impact. . . . As part of a balanced entertainment diet, the games can provide stress relief for kids, they can help with aspects of coordination and concentration on visual details, and they can help kids relate to one another in some forms of healthy competition.[20]

Someone who strongly disagrees that video games are harmful is Steve Pritchard, a game designer from the United Kingdom. Pritchard has been creating video games for more than 20 years. Although he believes that the most violent video games should be restricted to adult use and not played by children, he insists that blaming games for real-life problems is wrong. He explains:

> People who suggest that video games are harmful are applying a blanket statement to such a massive variety of product that it's hard not to

> " Although violent video games get more publicity than other types of games, many of the most popular games are not even rated for mature audiences. "

laugh. I've worked with hundreds of people in the video games industry, have designed maybe three dozen different games, and have met and talked to countless numbers of people that have played those games. And those I work with—very much like myself—have been playing video games for all of their adult life and most of their childhood. They've all had massive exposure to these games and not one of them shows any signs of having been harmed by them.[21]

Pritchard adds that video games are often criticized for their violence, but those games should not be everyone's focus. He says:

I've seen games where the object is for children to dress Barbie in a number of different princess costumes. One popular handheld games console allows its user to play with, feed, wash, and brush a virtual dog. Many of the titles for the Nintendo Wii are designed to encourage the whole family to get together and play games. Do these titles fall under the "harmful" banner? Of course they don't.[22]

What Kinds of Games Are Most Popular?

Although violent video games get more publicity than other types of games, many of the most popular games are not even rated for mature audiences. According to an industry report by the NPD Group, the top-selling video game of 2006 was *Madden NFL '07*, an E-rated game in which players assume the role of a football star, and the second-best seller was *New Super Mario Bros.*, which is also E-rated and is labeled with the descriptor "Comic Mischief." Nintendo entices video game enthusiasts with the following description of *New Super Mario Bros.*: "Run, jump, and stomp your way through raging volcanoes, tropical islands, snow-capped peaks, and unimaginable challenges! Grab a Mega Mushroom and grow to incredible proportions, or smash through your foes in a blue Koopa shell!"[23] The third top seller, *Gears of War*, was rated M, with content descriptors "Blood and Gore, Intense Violence, and Strong Language." Of the remaining top-10 sellers for 2006, 3 games were rated E, one was rated E10+, and 3 were rated T.

Video Games and Intelligence

Video game advocates are convinced that games stimulate players by enhancing intelligence and their ability to learn. Many games have been shown to help players develop complex problem-solving skills, learn to think logically and strategically, improve alertness, and become more tech savvy by gaining computer skills. Lee Wilson, an education and business consultant, touts the educational benefits of learning games such as *Oregon Trail, Civilization*, and *Quest Atlantis* and says that the most popular video games are extremely complex puzzles that succeed because "deep and difficult learning is fun in itself." He adds that there is an "impressive and growing international body of research documenting the learning impact modern video games can have."[24] Wilson believes that video games are such a valuable part of young people's learning that they should be integrated into educational curricula. He refers to the June 2007 National Educational Computing Conference, during which there were 18 sessions focusing on how to incorporate games into core curriculum areas, including reading, writing, algebra, history, art, physics, biology, and environmental studies, among others.

James Paul Gee agrees that video games are a valuable component of education. He says that the standard method of teaching and testing is outdated, as well as ineffective, in preparing kids for the future. "The evidence, as far as I can see, is that many young children today are learning more about art, design, and technology from their video games . . . than they are from our technologically impoverished schools." Gee emphasizes the importance of students having extraordinary technological knowledge, and he says that video games can play a major role in building that knowledge. He wants educators to take this issue seriously because he believes the future depends on it: "Natural disasters, global trade imbalances, and even international terrorism are problems where only the tech-savvy—only people who can link media, images, and design with science, math, and technology; only countries with people who can think about how to use new technologies in new ways—will survive."[25]

> "Video game advocates are convinced that games stimulate players by enhancing intelligence and their ability to learn."

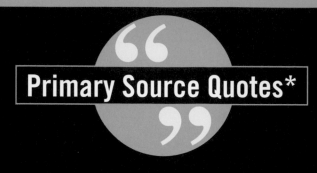

Are Video Games Harmful?

Primary Source Quotes

66 **Video games that allow players to kill real human beings are desensitizing generations of American society.** 99

—Mary Spio, quoted in Mike Snider, "Big-Selling War Games May Carry Bigger Cost," *USA Today*, June 9, 2004. www.usatoday.com.

Spio served in the U.S. Air Force during the first Gulf War and is now the editor of *One2One* magazine.

66 **No one has ever been able to prove through independent research that video games are harmful to children or to show that they cause violence.** 99

—Robert D. Richards and Clay Calvert, "Target Real Violence, Not Video Games," *Christian Science Monitor*, August 1, 2005. www.csmonitor.com.

Richards and Calvert are professors of communications and law at Penn State University and codirectors of the Pennsylvania Center for the First Amendment.

66 **Video game addiction has led some children to fail out of school, alienate themselves from everyone in their lives, and in extreme cases to commit suicide.** 99

—David Walsh, Douglas Gentile, Erin Walsh, and Nat Bennett, "Eleventh Annual Media Wise® Video Game Report Card," National Institute on Media and the Family, November 28, 2006. www.mediafamily.org.

Walsh, Gentile, Walsh, and Bennett are affiliated with the National Institute on Media and the Family.

Bracketed quotes indicate conflicting positions.

* Editor's Note: While the definition of a primary source can be narrowly or broadly defined, for the purposes of Compact Research, a primary source consists of: 1) results of original research presented by an organization or researcher; 2) eyewitness accounts of events, personal experience, or work experience; 3) first-person editorials offering pundits' opinions; 4) government officials presenting political plans and/or policies; 5) representatives of organizations presenting testimony or policy.

66 Games are not a panacea, and a child raised solely on games will definitely have a cartoonish view on life. But games really do have the power to teach things that textbooks, lectures and sports just don't. . . . [B]y allowing some games, and building on the lessons they impart, you will give your child the edge to succeed in the world just taking shape. 99

—John C. Beck and Mitchell Wade, "The Kids Are Alright: How Games Are Changing Our Kids for the Better," book summary, November 2006. www.gotgamebook.com.

Beck and Wade are coauthors of the book *The Kids Are Alright: How the Gamer Generation Is Changing the Workplace.*

66 Playing computer games affects children's behaviour in negative ways. The games are designed to be compulsive and addictive. 99

—Christopher Bantick, "Why Computer Games Should Worry Parents," *Age*, January 15, 2004. www.theage.com.au.

Bantick is a writer from Melbourne, Australia.

66 Blaming entertainment for social ills is nothing new, of course; Elvis Presley was accused of corrupting America's youth with lewd hip gyrations in the 1950s, for example, and in 1880s London the play 'Dr. Jekyll and Mr. Hyde' was blamed for encouraging Jack the Ripper in his crimes. 99

—Benjamin Radford, "Reality Check on Video Game Violence," *Live Science*, December 4, 2005. www.livescience.com.

Radford is managing editor of *Skeptical Inquirer* magazine and is the author of the book *Media Mythmakers: How Journalists, Activists, and Advertisers Mislead Us.*

66 As a parent, grandparent, and as a Member of Congress, I cannot sit quietly while these video games are poisoning our children's minds. . . . It is wrong that our children are being exposed to this kind of violence at an age when their minds and values are still being formed. 99

—Joe Baca, quoted in Laura C. O'Neill, "Baca Announces Creation of Congressional Sex and Violence in the Media Caucus at FTC Workshop" news release, October 29, 2003. www.house.gov.

Baca is a U.S. congressman from Rialto, California.

66 Video games are always used as a scapegoat for concerns. 99

—Guy Cumberbatch, quoted in BBC News, "Computer Games Do Have Benefits," July 15, 2005. http://news.bbc.co.uk.

Cumberbatch is the head of the Communications Research Group in the United Kingdom.

66 If your child, and in the case of the video games, it's still predominantly boys . . . [are] playing a game that encourages them to have sex with prostitutes and then murder them . . . that's kind of hard to digest and to figure out what to say, and even to understand how you can shield your particular child from a media environment where all their peers are doing this. 99

—Hillary Rodham Clinton, "Senator Clinton's Speech to Kaiser Family Foundation upon Release of *Generation M: Media in the Lives of Kids 8 to 18*," March 8, 2005. http://clinton.senate.gov.

Clinton is a U.S. senator from New York.

66 To say that [video game play] stimulates only evil is like saying reading the Bible or any other holy book stimulates only good. Reality is too complicated to blame polygons, moving pictures, or letters on a page. 99

—John Biggs, "Why Video Games Don't Cause Violence," CrunchGear, April 18, 2007. http://crunchgear.com.

Biggs is an author, consultant, and video game enthusiast from New York.

66 The more realistic and involving the game gets, and the greater the similarity between the action in the game and real life action, the stronger the negative effects would be. . . . These are subtle effects. . . . A teen isn't going to notice them. 99

—Joanne Cantor, quoted in Barbara F. Meltz, "Nintendo's Wii Game System Puts Violence in Motion," *Boston Globe*, June 23, 2007. www.boston.com.

Cantor is a research psychologist from Wisconsin who has studied the effects of media violence on children for 30 years.

66 If people have a criminal mind, it's not because they're getting their ideas from the video games. There's something much more deeply wrong with the individual. And it's not the game that's the problem. 99

—Doug Lowenstein, quoted in *60 Minutes*, CBS News, "Can a Video Game Lead to Murder?" June 17, 2005. www.cbsnews.com.

Lowenstein is the founder and former president of the Entertainment Software Association and now heads up an industry trade organization called The Private Equity Council.

Facts and Illustrations

Are Video Games Harmful?

- In 2006 worldwide spending on video games was more than **$31 billion**.

- Over **$7.4 billion** was spent on video games in the United States in 2006—almost triple the sales of 1996.

- According to the Entertainment Software Association, **69 percent** of American heads of households play video games regularly.

- The ESA says that the average age of video gamers is **30 years old** and that most have played video games for about 12 years.

- The National Institute on Media and the Family reports that almost **50 percent** of heavy video game players are from **6 to 17 years old**.

- In 2007 **24 percent** of Americans over 50 years old played video games, an increase from **9 percent** in 1999.

- According to the ESA, **62 percent** of video game players are male and **38 percent** are female. Women 18 and older represent a greater portion of the game-playing population (30 percent) than boys 17 and younger (23 percent).

Who Plays Video Games?

In June 2007 the Entertainment Software Association released its annual *Essential Facts About the Computer and Video Game Industry* report. The data were gathered by a market research firm that was contracted by the ESA. It is a targeted survey that includes data from more than 1,200 households in the United States that own either a video game console or a personal computer used to run entertainment software. Some of the findings are below.

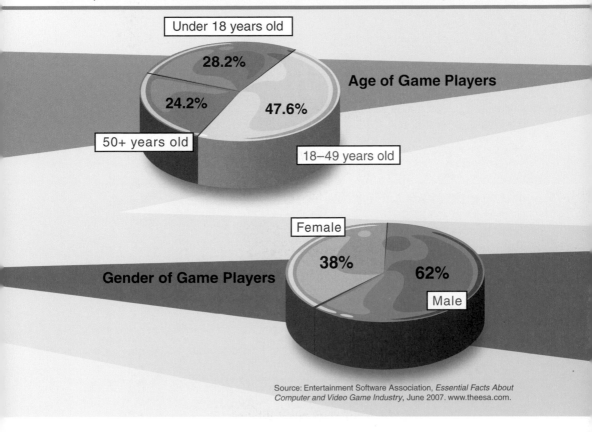

Source: Entertainment Software Association, *Essential Facts About Computer and Video Game Industry*, June 2007. www.theesa.com.

- A 2006 study by the Harvard School of Public Health showed that in the past 5 years, kids from ages 8 to 18 have nearly doubled the average amount of time they spend playing M-rated games **(from 26 to 49 minutes a day)**.

- *Forbes* magazine reports that of the **top-10 video games** in the United States during 2006, only one, *Gears of War*, was rated M.

Top-Selling Video Games in 2006

Included in the ESA's June 2007 report on video game usage was the following list of the top-selling video games for the year 2006. Although only three were rated Mature (M), two Teen (T) rated video games, and one rated Everyone (E10+) contained content descriptors that indicated violence and blood.

Rank	Title	Rating	ESRB content descriptors
1	Madden NFL 07 (PlayStation2)	E	none
2	New Super Mario Bros.	E	comic mischief
3	Gears of War	M	blood and gore, intense violence, strong language
4	Kingdom Hearts 2	E10+	mild blood, use of alcohol, violence
5	Madden NFL 07 (Xbox 360)	E	none
6	Final Fantasy XII	T	blood, realistic violence
7	Brain Age: Train Your Brain in Minutes a Day	E	none
8	Tom Clancy's Ghost Recon: Advanced Warfighter	T	blood, mild language, violence
9	NCAA Football 07	E	none
10	Guitar Hero II	T	mild lyrics
11	Grand Theft Auto: Liberty of City Stories	M	blood and gore, intense violence, strong language, strong sexual content
12	Grand Theft Auto: San Andreas	M	blood and gore, intense violence, strong language, strong sexual content

Source: Entertainment Software Association, *Essential Facts About Computer and Video Game Industry*, June 2007. www.theesa.com.

- In a March 2005 survey by the Kaiser Family Foundation, only about **20 percent of kids** reported that their parents had any rules for video game use.

Youth Video Game Addiction

In a January 2007 online poll conducted by the market research firm Harris Interactive, 1,178 young people aged 8 to 18 were surveyed to determine whether they were addicted to playing video games. Afterward, the firm reported that they had found a "national prevalence rate of pathological video game use among youth." The study also found that nationally, 8.5 percent of youth gamers can be classified as pathological or clinically "addicted" to playing video games. Nearly 23 percent of youth say that they have felt "addicted to video games," with 31 percent of males and 13 percent of females feeling "addicted." The graph below shows how many hours various youth groups play video games per week.

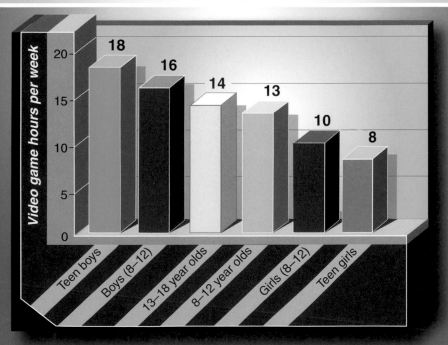

Source: Harris Interactive, "Video Game Addiction: Is It Real?" April 2, 2007. www.harrisinteractive.com.

Do Video Games Cause Violent Crime?

❝Our job is dangerous enough as it is without having our kids growing up playing those games and having the preconceived notions of 'let's kill an officer.' It's almost like putting a target on us.❞

—An unidentified police officer quoted in *60 Minutes*, "Can a Video Game Lead to Murder?"

❝Violence does not come from video games and people who claim their crimes are video game inspired are either finding a way out of prison or probably belong in a straitjacket to begin with.❞

—Brian O. Gonzalez, "Video Games Do Not Harm Children or Lead to Violence."

On June 7, 2003, 18-year-old Devin Moore was taken to a police station in Fayette, Alabama, on suspicion of stealing a car. He had no criminal history and was cooperative as Officer Arnold Strickland booked him—then suddenly Moore snapped, lunging at Strickland and grabbing his gun. He shot the officer twice. When Officer James Crump heard the shots and came running, Moore shot him three times, and then also shot a 911 dispatcher. On his way down the hall he grabbed a set of car keys and sped away in a stolen police cruiser. When he was later captured and arrested, police learned that he had spent hundreds of hours playing *Grand Theft Auto*, a video game in which players can decapitate police officers, shoot them with sniper rifles, hack them up with chainsaws, and set them on fire. In the game, players receive extra points for shooting cops in the head—which is what Moore did to his victims—all three of whom died. Afterward he reportedly told police, "Life is like a video game. Everybody's got to die sometime."[26] Because Moore's violent acts so closely mirrored the violence in the video game, attorney Jack Thompson spoke out, saying that the game was partly responsible.

Active Versus Passive Entertainment

Proponents of video games often argue that the games are no more influential than movies or television. In an article in the gaming Web site Ars Technica, Jonathan M. Gitlin writes:

> Although some people are worried about children's exposure to violent video games, they are just one of many forms of violent content that kids are exposed to these days. These games might be rated M for mature, yet the latest *Die Hard* movie, entertaining though it might be, is only rated PG-13 despite an awful lot of carnage, including a lengthy scene where Bruce Willis beats a woman half to death and then drops an SUV on her. If misogynistic violence is OK for the silver screen, why not the Xbox?[27]

The people who disagree with Gitlin's viewpoint say that video games are more influential because they have different effects on kids. Television and movies are passive entertainment, meaning that viewers watch them but do not interact with actors on the screen or participate in the action. Video games, however, are not passive. When kids play violent video games, they are actively involved in the violence. They are in charge of the controls and they have the power over their own characters, as well as all the other characters. Psychologist Craig Anderson explains:

> " **Proponents of video games often argue that the games are no more influential than movies or television.** "

We do think the violent video games are likely to have a bigger effect, mainly because of the active participation. You are practicing all the aspects of violence: decision-making and carrying it out. That is not the case in a television show or violent movie. You're not the one who decides to pull the trigger or tries to hurt someone; you're simply the observer. Practicing making a particular kind of decision, makes you better at making that kind of decision, just like practicing your multiplication tables makes you better at multiplication.[28]

Anderson adds that today's video games allow young people to participate in violent interactive entertainment that goes far beyond anything that has ever been available to them in television or movies. Some of these games, he says, "reward players for killing innocent bystanders, police, and prostitutes, using a wide range of weapons including guns, knives, flame throwers, swords, baseball bats, cars, hands, and feet."[29] He is convinced it is this interactive violence that can potentially lead to violent acts.

> "Kawashima's research showed that video game play affected the teenagers' frontal lobes, which he interpreted to mean that excessive game play could stunt brain development and interfere with a young person's ability to control negative behavior."

Tyler Staples, a West Michigan financial advisor and the father of two young children, disagrees that violent video games are responsible for real-life violence. He says that when young people commit violent acts, many factors influence their behavior. Video games alone cannot be blamed. Staples used to spend hours playing the video game *Grand Theft Auto: Vice City*, and while he admits that the game is "brutally violent," he enjoyed playing it. He found it to be an exciting, interactive form of entertainment. As he explains:

It was fun, but not because I really wanted to do any of

the things that the character was doing in the game. I never had the urge to snipe people, or to challenge law enforcement, or steal vehicles. To this day, I have never been in a fistfight, never been arrested, never shoplifted or stolen a car. I don't have a desire to do any of these things either, but it was fun in a fantasy world where people didn't really die and nobody really got hurt.[30]

Video Games and the Brain

Research conducted to attempt to show the correlation between violent video games and the human brain has resulted in some controversial findings. In 2001 brain-mapping expert Ryuta Kawashima and a team of researchers from Tohoku University in Japan investigated the levels of brain activity in young people who played violent video games. Hundreds of teenagers were involved in the study. The researchers compared brain scans from those who played the games with others doing a simple, repetitive arithmetical exercise that involved adding single-digit numbers for 30 minutes straight. They expected to find that kids benefited from the hours they spent playing video games, but the results of their research were actually quite different. They found that the video games only stimulated activity in the left hemisphere, the part of the brain associated with vision and movement.

> " Some people believe that the increase in juvenile crime is due in part to violent video games. "

Their biggest concern was what they could see happening in the frontal lobes of those who played the games. The frontal lobe of the brain plays an important role in helping to keep behavior in check, such as refraining from lashing out or exhibiting violent actions. But the brain's frontal lobes are not fully developed until people are about 20 years old, which is why it is not uncommon for children to act naughty or throw temper tantrums. Kawashima's research showed that video game play affected the teenagers' frontal lobes, which he interpreted to mean that excessive game play could stunt brain development and interfere with a young person's ability to control negative behavior. Kawashima later expressed his concern about these findings: "There is a problem we will have with a new generation of children—who play computer games—that we have never seen before. The implications are very serious for an increasingly violent society and these students will be doing more and more bad things if they are playing games and not doing other things like reading aloud or learning arithmetic."[31]

A more recent study was conducted in 2006 by researchers at the Indiana School of Medicine. They divided a group of 44 young people into 2 groups and randomly assigned them to play one of 2 games: *Need for Speed*, which is considered high-energy but nonviolent; and an ultraviolent first-person shooter game called *Medal of Honor: Frontline.* Immediately after the video game sessions, the participants' brains were scanned with magnetic resonance imaging (MRI) equipment. The researchers found that the brains of kids who played *Medal of Honor* for 30 minutes showed increased emotional arousal, with a corresponding decrease of brain activity in areas that affected self-control and attention. Those negative effects were not present in the kids who played *Need for Speed.* The research was funded by the Center for Successful Parenting, and the organization's director, Larry Ley, says the study serves as a warning for parents, who need to monitor closely what video games their children are playing: "There's enough data that clearly indicates that [game violence] is a problem. And it's not just a problem for kids with behavior disorders."[32]

While these types of studies have shown a link between violence and brain activity, they do not necessarily prove that video games make people more prone to violence than does other entertainment. John P. Murray, a psychology professor at Kansas State University, conducted research using the same type of brain scanning technology as the Indiana researchers. His subjects were a group of 40 teenagers, and when exposed to violent stimuli, their brains also showed emotional arousal. But they were not playing video games—they were watching short clips from the Sylvester Stallone boxing movie, *Rocky IV.*

Video Game Violence and Crime Trends

People who argue that video games do not cause real-life violence often support their viewpoint with crime trends. Violent video games have grown steadily more popular since they were first released in the early 1990s, while violent crime decreased during the same period. According to a September 2007 report by the Federal Bureau of Investigation (FBI), more than 1.9 million violent crimes were committed in the United States during 1991. In 2006 the number of violent crimes totaled just over 1.4 million, which represents a 26 percent reduction over 15 years.

As positive as those statistics are, however, violent crime rates in the short term have risen. After continuing on a downward trend from 1992 to 2004, violent crime spiked in 2005, and then went up again in 2006. The FBI also says that juvenile crime is on the rise. Between 2002 and 2006, the number of arrests for murders and manslaughters rose 4.5 percent—but the number of these violent crimes that were committed by kids under 18 years old rose nearly 18 percent. Also between 2002 and 2006, the number of robberies committed by juveniles rose 34.4 percent, and the number of weapons

> " When the kids were asked why they played these games, many said that violent video game play helped them manage their feelings, including anger and stress. "

arrests rose 31 percent. Some people believe that the increase in juvenile crime is due in part to violent video games. Game advocates, however, reject that notion as speculation, saying the most significant factor is the long-term decrease in crime. Jason Della Rocca, executive director of the Game Developers Association, explains: "These numbers quantitatively prove that (the idea of violence caused by video games) is hype-based and not based on any actual statistical progression toward violence. It's not supported by real-world data. It's more a soapbox for politicians."[33]

David Grossman, a psychologist and violence expert who trains elite military and law enforcement organizations all over the world, disagrees with Della Rocca's viewpoint. Grossman says that violent video games are training children to be violent and not feel any remorse for their actions. He points out that when police officers raid methamphetamine labs and gang hangouts, they often find that violent video games have been left behind. "Every time they take down a gang house, there's always one thing that will always be there. It's a video game. The video games are their newspaper, their television, their all-consuming narrative. And their video games are all cop-killer, criminal simulators."[34]

Can Video Games Curb Aggression?

Amidst all the controversy over video game violence, some people believe that playing violent video games is good for kids because it gives them an outlet for their anger and aggression. A young man named Tyrone from New York City says that he loves to play violent video games. One of his favorites is *Matrix Reloaded*, in which a special option called "focus" enables players to shoot characters and watch them die in slow motion. Tyrone says, though, that none of these games has ever made him want to hurt people in real life. He explains: "You could just go home and play *Grand Theft Auto* and come out refreshed. If you're mad, you can just play the game and run over people and kill people. . . . It's like an escape from reality."[35]

Many video game enthusiasts also say that violent games help them work off their aggression and anger. The June 2007 study at Massachusetts General Hospital's Center for Mental Health and Media involved 1,254 middle schoolers from two states. Of the participants, only 6 percent said they had not played any video games in the previous 6 months, and most seventh and eighth graders said that they regularly played violent video games. The most popular game among the boys surveyed was *Grand Theft Auto*, and that was the second-most popular game among the girls. When the kids were asked why they played these games, many said that violent video game play helped them manage their feelings, including anger and stress.

A game reviewer for DX Gaming whose screen name is Broadband says that violent video games are "perfect for virtual stress-relief." He adds that people who attack these games are self-important and uninformed because they forget that the most violent games were never designed for children to play: "Well, the Nintendo generation has grown up," he says. "We are adults, and play adult video games. Adult video games contain adult content and adult content often contains violence. Only the video game industry seems to be chastised for it, though."[36]

Primary Source Quotes*

Do Video Games Cause Violent Crime?

❝ Playing violent video games is to an adolescent's violent behavior what smoking tobacco is to lung cancer. ❞

—American Academy of Pediatrics (AAP) policy statement, quoted in Lori O'Keefe, "Media Exposure Feeding Children's Violent Acts, AAP Policy States," *AAP News*, January 2002. www.aap.org.

The AAP is composed of physicians who are committed to ensuring optimal physical, mental, and social health and well-being for all infants, children, adolescents, and young adults.

❝ Gang members don't commit drive-by shootings simply because they played a video game, nor do school kids shoot others simply because they played a video game. ❞

—Robert D. Richards and Clay Calvert, "Target Real Violence, Not Video Games," *Christian Science Monitor*, August 1, 2005. www.csmonitor.com.

Richards and Calvert are professors of communications and law at Penn State University and codirectors of the Pennsylvania Center for the First Amendment.

Bracketed quotes indicate conflicting positions.

* Editor's Note: While the definition of a primary source can be narrowly or broadly defined, for the purposes of Compact Research, a primary source consists of: 1) results of original research presented by an organization or researcher; 2) eyewitness accounts of events, personal experience, or work experience; 3) first-person editorials offering pundits' opinions; 4) government officials presenting political plans and/or policies; 5) representatives of organizations presenting testimony or policy.

66 Violence in video games appear[s] to have similar negative effects as viewing violence on TV, but may be more harmful because of the interactive nature of video games. 99

—Elizabeth Carll, quoted in American Psychological Association (APA) press release, "APA Calls for Reduction of Violence in Interactive Media Used by Children and Adolescents," August 17, 2005. www.apa.org.

Carll is a psychologist from New York City, a member of the Committee on Violence in Video Games and Interactive Media, and past president of the media division of the APA.

66 When I'm playing a video game, I might feel a little dirty: 'Ha-ha, I just killed you sucker.' But when I get out in real life, I would never think of doing those things. I know the difference between fantasy and reality. 99

—Terence McPherson, quoted in *Religion & Ethics*, PBS, "The Values in Video Games," May 30, 2003. www.pbs.org.

McPherson is a teenager and avid video game player from Silver Spring, Maryland.

66 When children witness violence, they are much more willing to inflict violence. Exposure to violence leads to violent behavior. 99

—Marcie Lightwood, quoted in Mariella Savidge, "Do Video Games Harm Young Boys?" *Morning Call*, March 20, 2006. www.mcall.com.

Lightwood is the program coordinator for Project Child, a child abuse prevention program in Allentown, Pennsylvania.

66 If you ever want to get geeks riled up, all you need to do is imply that video games cause violence. The response will be, well, violent. 99

—Annalee Newitz, "Blame Game," SFGate.com, January 14, 2002. www.sfgate.com.

Newitz is a writer from San Francisco, California.

66 Our kids are learning to kill, and learning to like it. 99

—David Grossman, "Teaching Kids to Kill," *Phi Kappa Phi National Forum*, Fall 2000. www.killology.com.

Grossman is a psychologist and violence expert who trains elite military and law enforcement organizations all over the world, as well as the author of *Stop Teaching Our Kids to Kill* and *On Killing*.

....

66 You get a group of teenage boys who shoot up a school— of course they've played video games. Everyone does. It's like blaming food because we have obese people. 99

—James Gee, quoted in Emily Sohn, "What Video Games Can Teach Us," Science News for Kids, January 21, 2004. www.sciencenewsforkids.org.

Gee is an education professor at the University of Wisconsin and the author of the book *What Video Games Have to Teach Us About Learning and Literacy*.

....

66 With violent video game play, children learn to associate violence with pleasure when they are rewarded for hurting another character, and this undermines moral sensitivity. 99

—Darcia Narvaez, quoted in Susan Guibert, "New Video Game 'Bully' as Harmful as Name Suggests," *Notre Dame ReSource*, November 17, 2006. http://al.nd.edu.

Narvaez is a psychologist at the University of Notre Dame.

....

66 The media in particular loves to bash video games, making sure to point out any time there's an Xbox within 50 yards of a crime. 99

—Duke Ferris, "Caution: Children at Play—the Truth About Violent Youth and Video Games," *Game Revolution*, October 19, 2005. www.gamerevolution.com.

Ferris owns the California company Net Revolution, Inc. as well as the Game Revolution Web site, and he lists his occupation as "Geek."

....

> 66 **The players of today's video games find themselves assuming the role of the most despicable people to walk the earth by carrying out mind-altering tasks with realistic graphics. These games reward and encourage violent criminal conduct.** 99

—Parents Television Council (PTC), "Violent Video Game Campaign." www.parentstv.org.

The PTC is an organization that seeks to educate parents about the negative effects of violent media, including video games, on children.

> 66 **No research has found that video games are a primary factor or that violent video game play could turn an otherwise normal person into a killer.** 99

—Henry Jenkins, "Reality Bytes: Eight Myths About Video Games Debunked," *The Video Game Revolution*, PBS, December 2005. www.pbs.org.

Jenkins is the director of comparative studies at the Massachusetts Institute of Technology.

Do Video Games Cause Violent Crime?

- In a 2004 study of 81 T-rated video games, Harvard researchers Kevin Haninger and Kimberly M. Thompson found that **90 percent** rewarded or required injuring of characters, and **69 percent** rewarded or required killing. There were a total of 11,499 character deaths in the 81 games, including 5,689 deaths of human characters.

- A June 2007 study by Massachusetts General Hospital's Center for Mental Health and Media showed that **most seventh and eighth graders** regularly play violent video games.

- According to the Federal Trade Commission (FTC), **42 percent** of unaccompanied 13- to 16-year-olds were able to purchase M-rated video games in 2006.

- In a 2007 report entitled **"Playing Video Games,"** the British Board of Film Classification ratings organization determined that video game violence is less influential and harmful to young players than violence in films or television.

- The ESA states that **85 percent** of all video games sold in 2006 were rated E, T, or E10+.

- After continuing on a steady downward trend from **1992 to 2004**, violent crime in the United States spiked in 2005, and then went up again in 2006.

- Between 2002 and 2006, the number of arrests for murders and manslaughters by kids under 18 years old rose by nearly **18 percent**.

- Between 2002 and 2006, the number of robberies committed by juveniles rose **34.4 percent**, and the number of weapons arrests rose **31 percent**.

Juvenile Crime Rises with Video Game Sales (2000–2006)

Since 2000, video game sales have increased 33 percent, from $5.6 billion in 2000 to $7.4 billion in 2006. The following table shows that some juvenile crime (committed by youth 18 years and younger) has increased during the same period of time.

Offense	2000	2001	2002	2003	2004	2005	2006
1. Murder and manslaughter	641	577	634	619	985	739	747
2. Robbery	15,310	12,799	14,927	14,645	16,276	16,791	20,555
3. Aggravated assault (inflicting serious bodily injury with or without a weapon)	20,133	19,563	21,438	22,573	25,848	26,834	28,060
4. Other assaults	35,307	34,116	37,055	35,221	38,038	36,967	36,589
5. Weapons: carrying, possessing, etc.	120,488	125,968	147,075	135,908	152,285	142,957	154,433

Sources: Entertainment Software Association, *Essential Facts About the Computer and Video Game Industry*, June 2007. www.theesa.com, and USDJ, FBI, *Crime in the United States, 2000–2007*. www.fbi.gov.

Mature (M)-Rated Video Game Sales to Children Decreasing

In an effort to monitor the effectiveness of the ESRB rating system, the Federal Trade Commission conducts regular undercover "mystery shops" to hundreds of retailers throughout the United States. According to the April 2007 FTC report *Marketing Violent Entertainment to Children*, the number of minors able to buy or rent M-rated video games has been significantly reduced. Retailers are also more likely to enforce ratings.

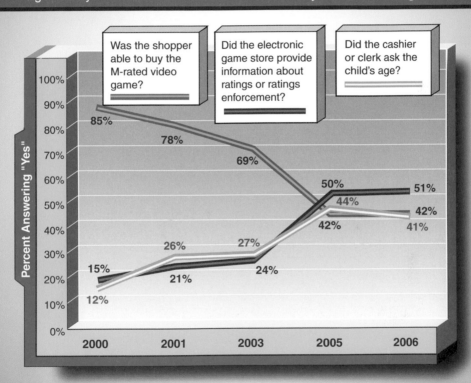

Source: Federal Trade Commission, *Marketing Violent Entertainment to Children*, April 2007. www.ftc.gov.

Which Video Games Are Most Violent?

The most violent video games are rated M, for Mature audiences, or AO, for Adults Only audiences. But even among these games, vast discrepancies in the amount of violence exists. According to an April 2007 review on the Web site DX Gaming, the following are the most violent video games of all time.

Rank	Title	Reviewer's comments
1	*Manhunt*	With weapons ranging from shards of glass to baseball bats to machetes to shotguns, Cash kills gang member after gang member in only the bloodiest of ways.
2	*Thrill Kill*	Senselessly violent? Probably.
3	*God of War*	In both the original and the sequel, gameplay in the *God of War* series is a sea of unrelenting violence.
4	*Gears of War*	The gore in *Gears of War* is as graphic as it comes.
5	*Soldier of Fortune*	With the amount of disfigurement encountered throughout *Soldier of Fortune*, anyone would agree that the name "gore zones" hit the nail right on the head.
6	*Killer 7*	Not only do bucket loads of blood spray out of enemies' bodies when they are killed, but the protagonist actually absorbs it to get stronger.
7	*The Punisher*	Bad guys are sawed, drilled, crushed, and fed to [piranhas], just to name a few of their undesirable fates.
8	*Grand Theft Auto* (all)	*Grand Theft Auto* games have become the poster children for violent video games.
9	*Mortal Kombat*	The granddaddy of video game violence, *Mortal Kombat* started it all.
10	*Loaded*	Look up the term "bloodbath" and you will find *Loaded* and its sequel, *Re-Loaded*.

Source: Review by "Broadband" for DX Gaming's Top 10 Most Violent Video Games," April 2, 2007. www.dxgaming.com.

How Do Video Games Affect Mental and Physical Health?

> " Children and adolescents can become overly involved and even obsessed with videogames. Spending large amounts of time playing these games can create problems and lead to poor social skills . . . lower grades and reading less; exercising less, and becoming overweight; aggressive thoughts and behaviors. "
>
> —American Academy of Child & Adolescent Psychiatry (AACAP), "Children and Video Games: Playing with Violence."

> " No one will argue that children shouldn't read books, play sport and invent imaginative creations out of blocks. It is time that electronic games are recognised as another form of entertainment that has the potential equally to aid a child's development as to harm it. "
>
> —Jason Hill, "Computer Games Can Be Good for Children."

Although the validity of video game research is sometimes questioned, most psychologists believe that the games can have positive as well as negative effects on mental and physical health. It depends, they say, on the types of games played and the amount of time spent playing them. Bill Vogler, executive director of the counseling organization Family Answers, shares his views: "Video games often get a bad rap.

I honestly do not think they are inherently bad, nor do they harm [kids] right out of the box. It's the excess, and potential for obsessive behavior that is the problem."[37]

Video Games and Physical Ailments

People who spend excessive amounts of time playing video games can suffer from a number of physical problems, including muscle cramps, back pain, bad posture, eye strain, and headaches. Another problem that is sometimes linked to video games is tendonitis, which is often called Nintendo thumb, joystick thumb, or Nintenditis. It is caused by keeping an intense grip on a game controller, repetitive button punching, and sharp wrist movements while guiding joysticks. According to the American Society of Hand Therapists, if precautions are not taken at an early age, children can suffer permanent damage to their hands and arms, developing long-term ailments such as tennis elbow, bursitis, or carpal tunnel syndrome. In early 2007 a hand therapist from Atlanta treated a 3-year-old boy who was suffering from painful muscle spasms in his hand. She learned that he was spending 2 to 3 hours every day playing computer games, and she determined that the spasms were caused by his extensive time using the joystick.

> People who spend excessive amounts of time playing video games can suffer from a number of physical problems, including muscle cramps, back pain, bad posture, eye strain, and headaches.

A more serious physical problem linked to excessive video game play is deep vein thrombosis (DVT), or blood clots. It is caused by a disruption in blood circulation and can form when someone sits in a cramped position for too long without getting up to move around. The clots usually form in the legs and are dangerous because they can break loose, travel through the bloodstream, and lodge in the lungs, causing permanent damage or death. Although these blood clots are most common in adults, they can and do happen in young people. In 2004 a 14-year-old British boy named Dominic Patrick developed DVT after spending 10 straight hours with his legs folded under him playing computer games. When he finally got up, he felt "pins and needles" in his legs, and one of his calves became badly swollen. Fortunately, he was hospitalized in time and doctors were able to treat him. His father later told a newspaper: "This just proves that DVT can affect even the fittest and healthiest of children."[38]

Video Games and Overweight Kids

One of the most common physical problems linked to video games is obesity, which is a serious health problem in the United States. More than 60 percent of Americans are considered overweight or obese, including an estimated 25 million children. Young people who spend excessive time playing video games and are not physically active often gain weight and lose muscle tone, although the same is true if they spend too much time on any sedentary activity, such as watching television.

CNNMoney writer Chris Morris cites a 1999 study that was done at University Hospital in Zurich, Switzerland, in which researchers found a strong connection between excessive video game play and childhood obesity. Their report stated that Swiss children who did not play video games had only a 6 percent chance of being overweight, while those who played for three hours every day had a 23 percent chance of being overweight. Morris does not disagree that the findings are correct; he just says that parents need to rely on common sense when their kids play video games. Says Morris:

> As with every kind of entertainment, most experts believe that the key is combining video game play with other types of activities in order to maintain a healthy balance.

> Basically, these researchers found if you sit on the couch all day, moving little but your thumbs, you won't get the proper amount of exercise. I ask you: Did it really take three M.D.s to figure this out? . . . Blaming video games

for obesity is nearly as ludicrous as blaming fast food restaurants. In either case, the solution to the problem is moderation. . . . It ain't rocket science, folks."[39]

As with every kind of entertainment, most experts believe that the key is combining video game play with other types of activities in order to maintain a healthy balance.

A Video Game Epidemic?

Video games are popular all over the world, but South Korea is considered the video game capital. South Korean game enthusiasts are especially fond of online, interactive role-playing games such as *StarCraft* and *Warhammer* that bring tens of thousands of players together via the Internet. There are 48 million people in South Korea, and an estimated 17 million people play these online games on a regular basis, either from their homes or in Internet cafes known as "PC baangs."

As more and more people in South Korea participate in online gaming, health officials have noticed a disturbing trend. According to a government-funded survey, an estimated 2.4 percent of people from ages 9 to 39 are addicted to video games, with another 10.2 percent classified as borderline cases at risk of addiction. In 2005 10 young South Koreans died from causes related to video game addiction, such as a disruption in blood circulation from sitting in a cramped position for too long. South Korean authorities are worried about what they are calling a video game addiction epidemic. Hundreds of private hospitals and psychiatric clinics throughout the country treat video game addicts, and the government launched a game addiction hotline in 2006. Health official Son Yeongi says that video game addiction is one of South Korea's "newest societal ills." He adds, though, that the blame for this health epidemic cannot be placed solely on video games. "Like anything, this is about excessive use."[40]

Therapists who have worked with compulsive video gamers say that the symptoms of addiction include sleep deprivation, disruption of normal daily life, and a loosening grip on reality. Kim Myung is a young South Korean man who became addicted to online interactive role-playing games. By the time he finally sought psychiatric counseling, he was playing the games from 8:00 A.M. until well after midnight every day.

"I guess I knew I was becoming addicted, but I couldn't stop myself," he says. "I stopped changing my clothes. I didn't go out. And I began to see myself as the character in my games."[41]

Photosensitive Epilepsy

The connection between video games and seizures was first discovered in Japan in 1997 after an alarming incident occurred. A cartoon called *Pocket Monsters*, later shortened to *Pokémon*, which was based on Nintendo's popular video game, was shown on television. About 20 minutes into the program an exploding "vaccine bomb" was set off, and the explosion caused five seconds of shooting, flashing red and blue lights. After watching it, hundreds of people, most of them children, suffered convulsions and were rushed to hospital emergency rooms. This incident triggered panic in Japan as health officials struggled to find out why it had happened. Some of the victims had previously been diagnosed with epilepsy, but many had never had seizures before.

Studies led researchers to discover a rare form of epilepsy known as photosensitive epilepsy, in which seizures are triggered by the brain's reaction to flashing lights at certain intensities, or to intense visual patterns. The research showed that television and video games could contribute to such light-induced seizures, although they were not the only sources. Seizures could also be triggered by natural phenomena such as sunlight shimmering on water or flickering through trees. Today the Epilepsy Foundation states that the likelihood of these types of seizures is extremely rare. The organization adds, however, that photosensitive people need to be aware of the possibility of seizure when using a computer, playing video games, or watching television. In order to inform the public about this potential risk, Nintendo posts the following warning on its Web site:

> " Therapists who have worked with compulsive video gamers say that the symptoms of addiction include sleep deprivation, disruption of normal daily life, and a loosening grip on reality. "

A very small portion of the population have a condition which may cause them to experience epileptic seizures or have momentary loss of consciousness when viewing certain kinds of flashing lights or patterns that are commonly present in our daily environment. These persons may experience seizures while watching some kinds of television pictures or playing certain video games. Players who have not had any previous seizures may nonetheless have an undetected epileptic condition.[42]

Therapeutic Video Games

Although video games have long been considered entertainment media, an increasing number of health care facilities throughout the United States are using them as part of their treatment plans. *U.S. News* health writer Betsy Streisand explains: "Long derided as the enemy of health for transforming children into weapon-loving, overweight zombies, computer games are now proving effective for everything from reducing pain and managing chronic disease to treating post-traumatic stress disorder and promoting fitness and exercise."[43]

At the Sister Kenny Rehabilitation Institute in Minneapolis, video games are used as part of a therapy regimen for patients who have suffered serious physical injuries. Therapists call this type of treatment "Wii-hab," named after Nintendo's popular Wii video game system. Patients play baseball, bowling, and tennis games, and even those with limited mobility have been able to use controls to relearn some bodily functions. According to occupational therapist Jennifer Smith, the Wii-hab program has helped spinal cord patients regain the ability to move so they are able to wash their faces, brush their teeth, get in and out of chairs, and start a car.

There are many other video games that are also designed to be part of patient therapy. More than 50 clinics around the United States use a video game system called S.M.A.R.T. BrainGames to help treat children and adults who have been diagnosed with attention deficit disorder (ADD). The Virtual Reality Medical Center in San Diego uses video games to treat phobias such as a fear of flying. Psychologists at the University of Victoria in British Columbia use a series of games called *Let's Face It!* to help children with autism learn facial recognition. The online video game *Brigadoon* helps people with a high-level form of autism known as Asperger's syndrome cope with their disease by practicing social skills in an anonymous environment.

"It's Stealth Learning"

Some health care facilities use video games with young cancer patients. A nonprofit organization in Palo Alto, California, called HopeLab developed a video game called *Re-Mission*, which is designed to help kids remain positive about their ability to fight their diseases. *Re-Mission* has 20 different levels, and its heroine is a gutsy, fully armed "nano-bot" named Roxxi. As rock music plays in the background, players guide Roxxi on her journey through the complex environment of the human body, controlling weapons such as the chemo blaster, the radiation gun, and the antibiotic rocket. These patients feel a sense of power as they use the weapons to blast away at deadly cancer cells and bacteria.

By playing *Re-Mission*, cancer patients learn how their disease progresses, as well as gain a better understanding of the importance of staying with the treatment plans prescribed by doctors. Sixteen-year-old Monzerratt Patino has been playing *Re-Mission* since she was diagnosed with a type of cancer called Hodgkin's lymphoma. She says that before she played the game, she did not realize how sick she could get if she neglected to take her medicine. Jeremy Hahn, a young bone cancer patient from San Francisco, says that playing *Re-Mission*

> An increasing number of health care facilities throughout the United States are using [video games] as part of their treatment plans.

helped him cope with difficult treatments. Taylor Carol, a 12-year-old leukemia patient from Dana Point, California, gained a better understanding of how cancer affected his body after playing the game. HopeLab's Steve Cole describes why such video games are successful with young cancer patients: "It's stealth learning. The things that happen inside the game don't stay in the game; they get in your head, and they change the way you approach the world. . . . Cancer is not death knocking on your door, but basically an opponent whose butt you are going to kick."[44]

A Video Game That Gets Kids Moving

One of the biggest criticisms of video games is that the people who play them sit still for hours at a time. But many new interactive fitness games, known as "exergames," are designed as entertainment that is physically motivating. One of the most popular exergame is *Dance Dance Revolution (DDR)*, in which players dance to lively music by using their feet to press four large, lighted arrows on a floor mat in an effort to match corresponding arrows on the screen. The game has more than 100 different songs, all at different skill levels, and players are scored and graded based on how accurately they step on the arrows. According to GameSpot reviewer Jeff Gerstmann, the newest video in the series *(Dance Dance Revolution Extreme)* is "a lot of fun and works especially well in a crowd, provided your crowd isn't filled with stuck-up dopes who think they're too good for a little silly dancing."[45]

DDR has been shown to provide workouts that are comparable to jogging or walking on Stairmaster machines. In 2006 researchers from the Mayo Clinic in Rochester, Minnesota, found that children playing *DDR* expended significantly more amounts of energy than children playing more sedentary video games or watching television. As a result, physical education classes all over the United States are integrating *DDR* into their routines. More than 40 schools in the Los Angeles area use *DDR*, as do schools throughout West Virginia and many other states. Robrietta Lambert, a West Virginia elementary school physical education teacher who regularly uses *DDR* in her classes, describes the video game's benefits: "It improves cardiovascular health as well as eye-hand coordination. Kids who don't like other things bloom on this. If they don't like basketball, jumping rope or ball activities, they like this."[46]

The Health Games Research Program

In November 2007 the Robert Wood Johnson Foundation (RWJF) invested $8.25 million to launch a program called Health Games Research, whose goal is to enhance the quality and effectiveness of interactive games that are used in health care. The program will enable researchers to gain a better understanding of the potential for video games to improve health, as well as help to develop relationships between game developers and health care experts. Financial grants will be awarded for the development of innovative video games that engage players in physical activity, as well as those that influence people's behaviors related to health, life-style choices, disease prevention, adherence to medical treatment plans, or management of disease. According to RWJF program officer Chinwe Onyekere, more research is needed to determine the long-term potential for video games in health care, but the outlook is promising. She says:

> While we have seen dramatic expansion within the health games field, we lack solid evidence to help identify when a game—used alone or in combination with other interventions—can improve people's health, and what specific difference it makes. Studies funded through *Health Games Research* will produce important, action-oriented results that will help this growing field make a meaningful difference in the health and health care of all Americans.[47]

Primary Source Quotes*

How Do Video Games Affect Mental and Physical Health?

People often go without sleep or skip meals to play video games. That can lower your immune system. It can also affect other areas of your life, like social interaction. Video games represent a form of escape from reality that can be dangerous. "

—Samuel Sharmat, quoted in Jennifer LeClaire, "Warning Signs Appear Along Road to Video Game Addiction," *TechNewsWorld*, September 13, 2006. www.technewsworld.com.

Sharmat is a psychiatrist in New York City whose subspecialty is treating addictions.

" Video games can provide valuable hand-eye coordination and develop skills of strategy and anticipation. You can play chess and, perhaps, develop some similar skills, but most kids prefer to be active and the video games fit the bill. "

—Patricia A. Farrell, quoted in Denise Mann, "Video Games and TV: Do They Make Kids Smarter?" WebMD, 2005. www.webmd.com.

Farrell is a clinical psychologist from Englewood Cliffs, New Jersey, a medical consultant, and the author of *How to Be Your Own Therapist*.

Bracketed quotes indicate conflicting positions.

* Editor's Note: While the definition of a primary source can be narrowly or broadly defined, for the purposes of Compact Research, a primary source consists of: 1) results of original research presented by an organization or researcher; 2) eyewitness accounts of events, personal experience, or work experience; 3) first-person editorials offering pundits' opinions; 4) government officials presenting political plans and/or policies; 5) representatives of organizations presenting testimony or policy.

❝I saw somebody this week who hasn't been to bed, hasn't showered . . . because of video games. He is really a mess.❞

—Karen Pierce, quoted in Lindsey Tanner, "Is Video-Game Addiction a Mental Disorder?" MSNBC, June 22, 2007. www.msnbc.msn.com.

Pierce is a Chicago psychiatrist who says she sees at least two children per week who play video games excessively and treats them as she would any other addict.

....

❝To understand why games might be good for the mind, begin by shedding the cliché that they are about improving hand-eye coordination and firing virtual weapons. The majority of video games on the best-seller list contain no more bloodshed than a game of Risk.❞

—Steven Johnson, "Your Brain on Video Games," *Discover*, July 24, 2005. http://discovermagazine.com.

Johnson is a columnist for *Discover* and *Wired* magazines and is the author of five books, including *Everything Bad Is Good For You: How Today's Popular Culture Is Actually Making You Smarter*.

....

❝There's a widespread but false belief that violent games are healthy because they allow kids a way of venting their aggression. They don't.❞

—Peter Lavelle, "Kids, Violence and Computer Games," *Pulse*, Australian Broadcasting Corporation, April 13, 2006. www.abc.net.au.

Lavelle is a physician and medical writer in Australia.

....

❝You could make lots of behavioral things into addictions. Why stop at video gaming?❞

—Michael Brody, quoted in Lindsey Tanner, "Is Video-Game Addiction a Mental Disorder?" MSNBC, June 22, 2007. www.msnbc.msn.com.

Brody is a psychiatrist and head of a TV and media committee at the American Academy of Child and Adolescent Psychiatry.

....

> **Researchers believe that electronic games are associated with an increased risk of childhood obesity and can cause overuse injuries of the hand.**

Better Health Channel, "Computer Games—Health Issues," October 2006. www.betterhealth.vic.gov.au.

The Better Health Channel is an online consumer health information resource that is part of the Department of Human Services of Victoria, Australia.

> **The current fad of pointing out how games are leading to bad health habits is missing the point. Parenting, good personal exercise habits, etc. are the keys to maintaining your health.**

—Ben Sawyer, quoted in Louis Bedigian, "Are Video Games Good for Your Health? The 2004 Games for Health Conference Looks for Answers," *GameCube News*, June 21, 2004. http://gamecube.gamezone.com.

Sawyer is a video game designer, president of Digitalmill, and the founder of the Games for Health project.

> **Sedentary kids are more likely to gain weight because they don't burn calories through physical activity. Inactive leisure activities, such as watching television or playing video games, contribute to the problem.**

—Mayo Clinic, "Childhood Obesity," March 31, 2006. www.mayoclinic.com.

Mayo Clinic is the largest integrated nonprofit health care practice in the world.

> **People want to know if a video game is good or bad and the position we take is it's neither good nor bad—it's what you do with it.**

—James Paul Gee, quoted in Daisy Whitney, "Video Games: Friend or Foe?" DisneyFamily.com. http://family.go.com.

Gee is an education professor at the University of Wisconsin and the author of the book *What Video Games Have to Teach Us About Learning and Literacy.*

66 They [play video games] to the exclusion of other activities, and kids' attention spans become shorter, and some of the content of these video games is really way inappropriate and not psychologically healthy. **99**

—Rebecca Kiki Weingarten, quoted in Denise Mann, "Kids Playing: Slingshots vs. Video Games," Health & Parenting, WebMD. www.webmd.com.

Weingarten is a psychotherapist and the cofounder/coach of Daily Life Consulting in New York City.

66 I think the biggest thing to do isn't to limit the gaming itself, but to decide what else a child should be doing besides playing games that are musts . . . homework, playing outside, watching the news, etc. . . . If they're doing the other things in their 'activity diet' then I don't see a problem. **99**

—Ben Sawyer, quoted in "Dr. Pac-Man? Smart and Healthy Video Games," *Connect for Kids*, July 13, 2005.

Sawyer is president of the consulting firm Digitalmill and is the author of several books on video games and game development.

How Do Video Games Affect Mental and Physical Health?

- According to research by the National Institute on Media and the Family, children who spend more time playing video games are heavier and are more likely to be classified as **overweight or obese**.

- As video games have grown in popularity, obesity among America's youth has increased. The American Obesity Association says that **30.3 percent** of children ages 6 to 11 are overweight, and **15 percent** are obese; for teens, the rate is almost identical.

- Health care officials in South Korea say that **2.4 percent** of people from ages 9 to 39 are addicted to video games and another **10.2 percent** are considered borderline cases at risk of addiction.

- According to the Epilepsy Foundation, the brightly flashing lights and vivid graphics in some video games can be one cause of seizures among young people who have **photosensitive epilepsy**.

- An increasing number of **health care facilities** are using video games as part of their treatment programs.

- In 2006 researchers at the University of Rochester determined that the eyesight of people who played certain action-oriented video games for **a few hours a day** over the course of a month showed a 20 percent improvement in their vision.

Video Game Usage and Childhood Obesity Rising

Video games designed for home use were first introduced in the 1970s. As fancier game consoles, computers, and video games have become available, the popularity of these games has grown at a steady pace. According to the National Institute on Media and the Family, the amount of time young people spend playing video games continues to increase— and the prevalence of obesity among children and adolescents in the United States has also steadily increased.

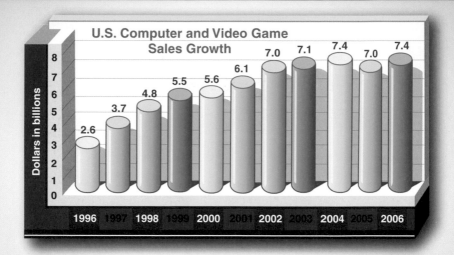

U.S. Computer and Video Game Sales Growth (Dollars in billions): 1996: 2.6, 1997: 3.7, 1998: 4.8, 1999: 5.5, 2000: 5.6, 2001: 6.1, 2002: 7.0, 2003: 7.1, 2004: 7.4, 2005: 7.0, 2006: 7.4

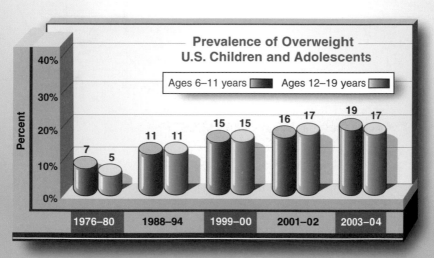

Prevalence of Overweight U.S. Children and Adolescents (Percent): Ages 6–11 years, Ages 12–19 years. 1976–80: 7, 5; 1988–94: 11, 11; 1999–00: 15, 15; 2001–02: 16, 17; 2003–04: 19, 17

Source: David Walsh et al., National Institute on Media and the Family, *Eleventh Annual Mediawise® Video Game Report Card*, November 28, 2006. www.mediafamily.org, and Trust for America's Health, http://healthyamericans.org.

Video Games and Physical Ailments

Many health care experts have linked excessive video game play with a number of physical ailments. Back pain, muscle cramps, and bad posture can result from spending hour after hour sitting in one position in front of the computer, television screen, or video game console. Headaches, often caused by eye strain, are extremely common among avid video game and computer game enthusiasts, and can be triggered by staring at the screen for a long period of time without giving the eyes proper rest. Tendinitis (often called Nintendo thumb, joystick thumb, or Nintenditis) is a repetitive strain injury (RSI) that is caused by keeping an intense grip on a game controller, repetitive button pushing, and sharp movements of the wrist. Tendons are the tough cords of tissue that connect muscles to bones. Although tendinitis can affect any tendon, it is most common in the wrist and fingers, and causes swelling and pain. Continued stress on tendons, nerves, and ligaments, can lead to long-term problems such as tennis elbow, bursitis, or carpal tunnel syndrome.

Headache

Eye strain

Tendinitis

Back pain

Source: American Society of Hand Therapists, "ASHT Focuses on Hand Therapy Awareness and Injury Prevention Week, June 11–15, 2007," June 12, 2007. www.asht.org. David Walsh et al., National Institute on Media and the Family, *Eleventh Annual Media Wise® Video Game Report* Card, November 28, 2006. www.mediafamily.org.

- A 2005 study of overweight and average weight children by researchers at Liverpool Hope University (United Kingdom) determined that the video game *Dance Dance Revolution* increased players' heart rates so that they obtained an aerobic workout and gained cardio-physical benefits, even at the easiest levels of the game.

How Violent Video Games Affect the Brain

In a 2006 study by the Indiana School of Medicine at Indianapolis, researchers found that playing violent video games may result in lingering effects on brain function. Dr. Vincent P. Mathews led the research, which involved 44 males and females under the age of 18. Half were randomly assigned to play a violent video game, while the others played a nonviolent video game, both for 30 minutes at at time. In Mathews's study, the researchers could see distinct differences in brain activity between the two groups. Compared to subjects who played nonviolent video games, those who played the violent games showed decreased activity in the prefrontal part of the brain, which governs inhibitions, concentration, and self-control.

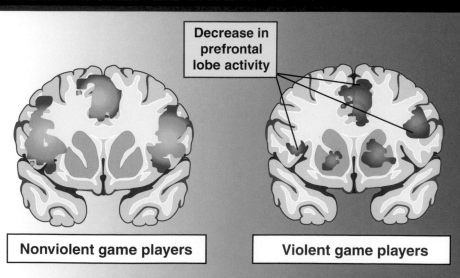

Decrease in prefrontal lobe activity

Nonviolent game players   **Violent game players**

Source: Radiological Society of North America (RSNA), "Violent Video Games Leave Teenagers Emotionally Aroused," November 28, 2006. www.rsna.org.

Should Video Games Be Regulated?

66 We prohibit children from smoking. We regulate driver's licenses. We prohibit alcohol. We prohibit lots of things from children, and we think it's logical that kids should not be able to purchase these games on their own. 99

—Adam Keigwin, quoted in Seth Schiesel, "Courts Block Law on Video Game Violence."

66 The most powerful case against government regulation or censorship of video games is that it's none of government's business. In a free society, parents should decide what their children see, hear, or play; Uncle Sam should not serve as a surrogate parent. 99

—Adam D. Thierer, "Regulating Video Games: Parents or Uncle Sam?"

The debate over video game regulation began in the early 1990s, after game designers Ed Boon and John Tobias released a new arcade game called *Mortal Kombat*. With its mysterious, medieval setting, mythical characters, and digitized graphics, it was unlike any game that had been developed before, and game enthusiasts loved it. But *Mortal Kombat* was different from other video games in another way—its unprecedented portrayal of lifelike, gory violence. Elaborate fight scenes gave players the ability to land deadly punches against opponents, spraying animated blood and sending characters flying through the air, as well as the ability to kill in gruesome ways. Steven L. Kent describes this in *The Ultimate History of Video Games:* "Fatalities ranged from Kano wrenching his opponents' hearts out of their chests to Scorpion pulling out their spines and skulls."[48]

The home version of *Mortal Kombat* was released in September 1993, and its popularity skyrocketed. Soon after the game went on sale to the public, U.S. Senator Joseph Lieberman became aware of it and grew concerned about the availability of such violent entertainment to children. He helped organize a series of panel discussions and hearings, during which the issue of video game violence was debated. One statement by the National Education Association's vice president, Robert Chase, was especially harsh: "Electronic games, because they are active rather than passive, can do more than desensitize impressionable children to violence. They actually encourage violence as the resolution of first resort by rewarding participants for killing one's opponents in the most grisly ways imaginable."[49] The hearings lasted for many months and resulted in the formation of two organizations: The Interactive Digital Software Association (later renamed the Entertainment Software Association), which served as the interactive entertainment industry's trade and lobbying association; and the Entertainment Software Rating Board, an independent organization that was charged with rating games.

How ESRB Ratings Are Assigned

Although video game developers are not required by law to submit their games to the ESRB, they know it is in their best interest to do so because many major retailers refuse to carry games that do not have ESRB ratings on the box. According to the ESRB's advertising guidelines (known as Ad Code), game development companies must include rating information on product packaging and in all game advertising.

To obtain ratings for their games, developers must submit an application to the ESRB that provides information about the content of the games, such as violence; offensive language; use of drugs, alcohol, or tobacco; and sexual or suggestive scenes. Along with the application, companies must include a DVD that shows the game's most extreme content. Three raters, working independently from each other, review the footage and then make separate recommendations to the ESRB's ratings department about the rating and content descriptors they feel are most appropriate. To ensure the integrity of the rating process, the identities of the raters are kept secret. Once a rating has been issued, the video game company must submit a final version of the game, along with the packaging with the rating and descriptors clearly marked, to the ESRB. If the ESRB discovers that a company has not accurately disclosed a game's content, the penalties can be severe: fines of up to $1 million and/or a refusal to rate the game. To say the least, developers are well aware that any attempt to deceive the ESRB is unwise.

How Effective Is the Rating System?

People in the entertainment industry, including video game developers, believe that the system of ESRB self-regulation is working very well. The Federal Trade Commission's April 2007 "Marketing Violent Entertainment to Children" report stated that the video game industry was in compliance with its voluntary standards regarding the display of ratings on product packaging. Senator Lieberman, who was instrumental in the development of the ratings system, has stated his belief that the system is effective, as he explained during a press conference in December 2006: "I have long said that the ESRB ratings are the most comprehensive in the media industry. There are many age-appropriate games that are clever and entertaining. Parents should understand and use the ratings to help them decide which video games to buy for their families."[50]

> " Although video game developers are not required by law to submit their games to the ESRB, they know it is in their best interest to do so. "

Not everyone agrees that the current rating system is a good one, however. Because the entertainment industry is responsible for its own activities and has no outside monitoring or laws that it must adhere to, Common Sense Media calls the system "the fox guarding the chicken coop."[51] One common complaint is that ESRB raters do not actually play the video games;

they just view the video footage that is provided by game developers. Some people argue that because the raters do not examine entire games, this can lead to erroneous ratings and to omissions and inconsistencies in content descriptors.

Harvard researchers Kevin Haninger and Kimberly M. Thompson became concerned about whether content descriptors were accurate, so they did a study and published their findings in the February 18, 2004, issue of the *Journal of the American Medical Association*. After creating a database of nearly 400 T-rated video games (rated for players aged 13 and older),

> "One common complaint is that ESRB raters do not actually play the video games; they just view the video footage that is provided by game developers."

Haninger and Thompson randomly chose 81 of the games to assess, and then compared the content they observed with the content descriptors assigned by the ESRB. They concluded that some of the most popular T-rated games featured content that was not indicated on the box, such as drug use, alcohol use, blood, and violence. In their follow-up report, they stated that because this content was not noted in the descriptors, the young people playing the games, as well as their parents, could be caught off guard by questionable content they were not expecting.

The Role of Retailers

According to organizations such as Common Sense Media, the National Institute on Media and the Family, and the Interfaith Center for Corporate Responsibility (ICCR), one of the most serious problems with the current ESRB system is that retailers are not legally bound to abide by the ratings. By law, they are not even required to check identification, and there are no legal penalties for those who sell or rent M- or AO-rated video games to children. The organization claims that most stores do not bother to check whether games are age-appropriate for purchasers. Adding to the problem, says the ICCR, is that many adult-rated video games are sold in toy stores, often on shelves next to children's games. Jack Brouse, who is the ICCR's "video game guru," says, "The controls aren't working." Brouse cites an investigation in 2005 by the New York City Council that revealed a "disturbing number of stores"[52] were selling adult video games to minors and were doing so knowingly. The investigation found that underage kids were able to buy adult games in 88 percent of the stores surveyed in New York City.

According to the FTC, however, there has been substantial improvement in the practices of retailers who sell and rent video games. Undercover "mystery shopping" visits in 2000 found that 85 percent of children aged 13 to 16 were able to buy M-rated games; by 2006 that number had dropped to 42 percent. Despite the lack of legal requirements, most major retailers have their own policies in place to abide by ESRB ratings, and they do so voluntarily. This was strengthened in November 2005 with the formation of the ESRB Retail Council, an organization composed of most major video game retailers, including Best Buy, GameStop, Blockbuster Video, Circuit City, Sears/K-Mart, Target, Toys "R" Us, and Wal-Mart. Members of the council pledged to restrict sales of M-rated games to people over the age of 17, as well as support semiannual unannounced, undercover visits to monitor their compliance. In June 2007 a new initiative was launched to make the system work even better. The ESRB announced its commitment to ongoing education of 10,000 independent and small chain retailers about ESRB ratings and the importance of not selling or renting mature-rated video games to people under the age of 17.

> According to the FTC . . . there has been substantial improvement in the practices of retailers who sell and rent video games.

Do Parents Pay Attention to Ratings?

In its "2007 Essential Facts About the Computer and Video Game Industry" report, the ESA states that 86 percent of game players in America under the age of 18 say they get their parents' permission when buying or renting video games, and 91 percent say that their parents are with them when they buy games. In a 2006 poll by the FTC, 87 percent of parents surveyed said they were aware of the ESRB rating system; 63 percent said they were familiar with the system, including the rating icons and content descriptors; 61 percent said they used rating icons most or all of the time; and 54 percent said they paid attention to content descriptors most or all of the time.

Yet not all surveys have yielded such positive results. According to the National Institute on Media and the Family, "Other research, including ours, does not paint quite such a rosy picture. In our sample of 1,430 third-, fourth-, and fifth-grade children and their parents, we find that parents and children have very different perceptions of how involved parents are." The organization refers to "an

> In spite of the unsuccessful efforts at video game legislation, those who are in favor of it vow to keep fighting because they see major flaws in the video game industry's self-regulatory system.

alarming gap between what kids say about the role of video games in their lives and what parents are willing to admit," and cites that while 73 percent of parents reported that they always help decide what video games their children buy or rent, only 30 percent of children said their parents do. When asked how often parents talk to their children about the video games they play, 51 percent of the kids said never, while only 5 percent of the parents said that. The survey concluded with the following statements: "These findings, and the gap between them, are basically identical to the national averages found in other studies. This suggests that parents may provide overly optimistic responses about their awareness of children's video game habits and their use of the ratings."[53]

The Role of the First Amendment

Because of the lack of legislation governing video game sales and rentals to minors, some states have attempted to pass their own laws—and one by one, their efforts have been struck down. Since 2001 federal judges have cited the Constitution's protection of free speech to reject attempts to regulate video games in a number of states, including California, Washington, Illinois, Michigan, Minnesota, Louisiana, and Missouri. In addition, the ESA has attempted to recover attorney fees and court costs for the cases it has fought, and it has been largely successful in doing so. One of the most notorious cases was in 2006, after the state of Illinois passed a law that made it illegal to sell violent and sexually explicit video games to minors. The ESA challenged the law and won. The judge declared the law unconstitutional and ordered the state to pay more than $500,000 in ESA's legal fees.

An attempt at national legislation, known as the Family Entertainment Protection Act (FEPA), was introduced in November 2005 by Senator Hillary Clinton and was cosponsored by Joseph Lieberman and other senators. Under FEPA, fines of up to $1,000 would be imposed on anyone selling an M- or AO-rated video game to a minor, with the fine jumping to as much as $5,000 for a second offense. Another part of the bill was an FTC investigation to determine whether the ESRB has been properly rating video games. FEPA did not become law, however. After being referred to a congressional committee for review, it expired without further action. Adam Thierer, who has written extensively against video game regulation, explains his views on why such legislation is wrong:

> Government regulation could easily cross the line into censorship. If legislators threaten [the] industry with fines or prosecution for mislabeling games, voluntary labeling will likely be abandoned altogether. Parents would lose access to valuable, reliable, and credible information about the age-appropriateness and content of the games they're thinking of buying. Of course, if [the] industry responded to such proposals by abandoning voluntary ratings, lawmakers would . . . propose a mandatory rating-and-labeling scheme instead. The courts would not allow legislators to regulate books or magazines in this manner, and there is no reason why video games should be any different.[54]

In spite of the unsuccessful efforts at video game legislation, those who are in favor of it vow to keep fighting because they see major flaws in the video game industry's self-regulatory system. David Grossman explains:

> Simply put, we need to work toward "legislation" which outlaws violent video games for children. . . . There is no

Constitutional "right" to teach children to blow people's heads off at the local video arcade. And we are very close to being able to do to the media, through "litigation," what is being done to the tobacco industry, hitting them in the only place they understand—their wallets.[55]

A Never-Ending Debate

Contentious discussions rage on about whether video games are harmful or beneficial, addictive or destructive, responsible for aggressiveness and violent acts or nothing more than entertainment. Parental watchdog organizations and some lawmakers persist in trying to pass legislation that will regulate the sale of mature-rated video games so they cannot legally be sold or rented to minors, but those efforts have been unsuccessful. If more people become concerned about possible connections between violent crime and video game violence, there will likely be increased pressure on game makers and possibly more lawsuits against them. Whether this will affect the types of video games that are created or how games are rated is unknown. In fact, all that is known with any certainty is that the controversy over video games will not easily be resolved, now or in the near future.

Should Video Games Be Regulated?

> ❝ You can hide behind the protections offered by the Constitution—which is every American's right—and maybe a smart lawyer will win the case. That still doesn't explain why the common denominator of quality has to begin in the gutter—and work down from there. . . . Surely the best creative minds of this generation can do better. ❞

—Charles Cooper, "Perspective: Why Don't Game Developers Get It?" CNET News.com, October 7, 2005. www.news.com.

Cooper is executive editor of commentary for CNET News.com.

> ❝ The definition of art isn't whether we like it. There are paintings that people regard as trash, there are books that people regard as trash, but we regard them as protected nonetheless. ❞

—Doug Lowenstein, quoted in Kristina Nwazota "Judge Weighs Ban on Violent Video Game Sales," *NewsHour*, PBS, July 16, 2003. www.pbs.org.

Lowenstein is the founder and former president of the Entertainment Software Association and now heads up an industry trade organization called The Private Equity Council.

Bracketed quotes indicate conflicting positions.

* Editor's Note: While the definition of a primary source can be narrowly or broadly defined, for the purposes of Compact Research, a primary source consists of: 1) results of original research presented by an organization or researcher; 2) eyewitness accounts of events, personal experience, or work experience; 3) first-person editorials offering pundits' opinions; 4) government officials presenting political plans and/or policies; 5) representatives of organizations presenting testimony or policy.

66 The ratings system already has become its own form of censorship as parents, too lazy, too busy or too un-involved to use their own judgment, rely on it for more than advice. Rather than make their own decisions about what their children can or should watch, these parents have empowered ratings panels to do their jobs for them. 99

—Igniq, "Opinion: Say 'No' to Family Entertainment Protection Act," December 18, 2005. www.igniq.com.

Igniq is a group of international video game enthusiasts who provide news reports, reviews, opinion pieces, and advice about gaming experiences.

66 We protect our children from buying inappropriate movies and ought to be able to protect them from buying inappropriate video games as well. 99

—Arnold Schwarzenegger, quoted in Jim Christie, "Schwarzenegger Appeals Ruling on Video Game Law," Reuters, September 5, 2007. www.reuters.com.

Schwarzenegger is the governor of California.

66 If the gaming industry is held to a standard much, much higher than that applied to other arms of the entertainment industry, and if this takes place without any proof whatsoever regarding the detrimental effects of gaming on youths . . . we'll see a whole new discussion on constitutionality, because the industry and related interests . . . will fight it tooth and nail. 99

—Ken Fisher, "Thompson Calls FEPA Unconstitutional," Ars Technica, December 12, 2005. http://arstechnica.com.

Fisher is editor in chief and writer for Ars Technica (Latin for the "art of technology"), an online news forum that specializes in editorials, reviews, analysis of technology trends, and expert advice on technology-related topics.

"Pediatricians and psychologists have been warning us that violent video games are harmful to children. I'm optimistic that the courts will heed their warnings."

—Mary Lou Dickerson, quoted in "Violent Video Games Under Attack," *Wired*, July 14, 2004. www.wired.com.

Dickerson is a congresswoman from the state of Washington who proposed a federal law that would ban the sale of some violent games to kids.

"This is all about protecting our children until they are old enough to protect themselves."

—Rod Blagojevich, quoted in Peter Slevin, "A Push to Restrict Sales of Video Games," *Washington Post*, December 16, 2004. www.washingtonpost.com.

Blagojevich is the governor of Illinois and a proponent of legislation that would ban the sale of certain video games to minors.

"How exactly do you legislate to guard against the real problem—lousy parenting?"

—Sue Ontiveros, "It's Up to Parents to Police Children's Video Game Choices," *Chicago Sun-Times*, January 8, 2005. http://findarticles.com.

Ontiveros is a columnist for the *Chicago Sun-Times* newspaper.

"People have been working very hard to stamp out bullying and now we have a game called *Bully*. This flags up a very important issue, that the computer games industry is not fully regulated. There needs to be an independent watchdog regulating the production of such games."

—Giselle Pakeerah, quoted in Ainsley Newson, "Children 'Made More Aggressive by Video Games,'" *Times*, (London) August 20, 2005. http://timesonline.co.uk.

Pakeerah is a mother from the United Kingdom who blames violent video games for the murder of her 14-year-old son, Stefan, in February 2005.

❝If you start saying that we're going to sue people because one individual out there read their book or played their game and decided to become a criminal, there is no stopping point. It's a huge new swath of censorship that will be imposed on the media.❞

—Paul M. Smith, quoted in *60 Minutes*, CBS News, "Can a Video Game Lead to Murder?" March 6, 2005. www.cbsnews.com.

Smith is a First Amendment lawyer in Washington, D.C.

❝We . . . advocate strongly for more stringent regulations regarding the sale and marketing of these games to minors for whom repeated play of these games poses a major public health concern.❞

—Common Sense Media, "Violent Video Games and Our Kids: A Common Sense Approach," May 2, 2005. www.commonsensemedia.org.

Common Sense Media is an organization that is dedicated to improving media and entertainment choices for families and children.

❝The debate over video-game regulation is being driven by myths and misperceptions. Policymakers and critics should consider the facts before moving forward with efforts to regulate the gaming industry, especially since such rules could have profound First Amendment implications as well.❞

—Adam Thierer, "Natural Born Regulators," *National Review Online*, March 29, 2006. http://nationalreview.com.

Thierer is director of the Progress in Freedom Foundation's Center for Digital Media Freedom in Washington, D.C.

Should Video Games Be Regulated?

- *Mortal Kombat*, released in 1992, was **the first video game** to depict graphic violence and bloodshed and is often called the granddaddy of violent video games by avid gamers.

- The Entertainment Software Association was **formed in 1994** as the Interactive Digital Software Association.

- The **Entertainment Software Rating Board** was formed in 1994.

- Although retailers **are not required by law** to adhere to ESRB ratings, most of the larger ones do so voluntarily and have policies in place to ensure compliance.

- According to the Federal Trade Commission, undercover "mystery shopping" visits in 2000 found that **85 percent** of children aged 13 to 16 were able to purchase M-rated games; in 2006 that number had dropped to **42 percent**.

- Numerous states have tried to pass laws that would make it illegal to sell or rent **M-rated video games** to minors, but all have been struck down by the courts.

Video Game Legislation

A number of states and local legislative bodies have tried to pass laws that would regulate video games. Most of these efforts have not been successful as federal courts have ruled that video games are protected under the United States Constitution and any attempt to ban or limit access to them is a violation of the First Amendment. The following are some recent attempts at video game legislation that were ruled unconstitutional.

Minnesota 2006

Proposed Minnesota Video Games Act would penalize minors for the purchase or rental of an M- or AO-rated game

Washington 2004

State law prohibited the sale of video games that depicted violence against law enforcement officers

Illinois 2005

Violent Video Games Law and Sexually Explicit Video Games Law

Michigan 2006

Proposed law to make it illegal to ban the sale of violent video games to minors

California 2005

Proposed law to make it a crime to knowingly sell or rent certain video games to minors

Louisiana 2006

Proposed law that would ban the sale of violent video games to minors

Oklahoma 2006

Proposed statute to prohibit the sale of video games depicting "inappropriate" violence to minors

St. Louis County, Missouri 2003

County ordinance made it unlawful to knowingly sell, rent, or make available violent video games

Americans' View of Government Video Game Regulation

A fall 2007 survey by the New York public relations firm Hill & Knowlton found that a majority of American consumers support regulation of video game sales. The survey, which was conducted online September 17–19, 2007, involved 1,147 adults over the age of 18. When asked if the government should regulate the sale of games with violent or mature content, 60 percent said yes, while a slim majority (51 percent) said that the government should regulate the content itself.

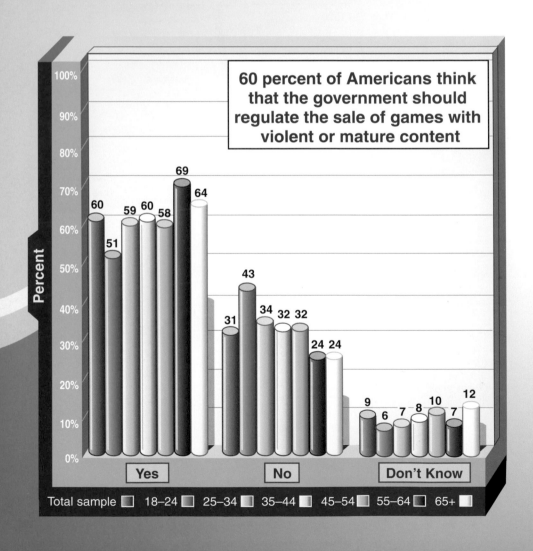

60 percent of Americans think that the government should regulate the sale of games with violent or mature content

Total sample ☐ 18–24 ☐ 25–34 ☐ 35–44 ☐ 45–54 ☐ 55–64 ☐ 65+ ☐

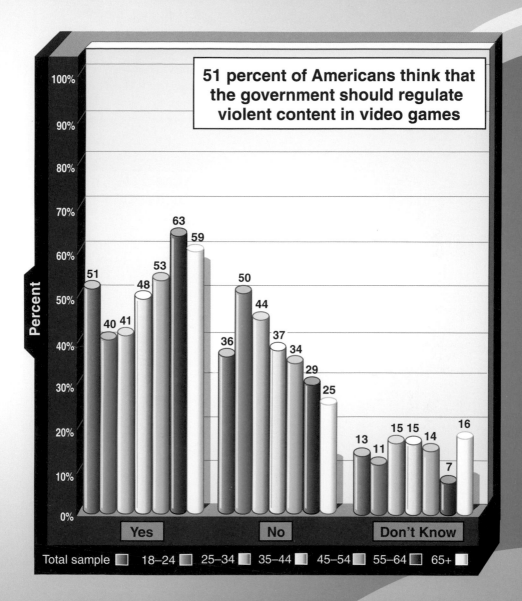

51 percent of Americans think that the government should regulate violent content in video games

Source: Hill & Knowlton, "Video Gaming Survey Results," December 5, 2007. www.hillandknowlton.com.

What Do Video Game Ratings Mean to Parents?

According to a 2006 study by Peter D. Hart Research Associates, which was commissioned by the ESRB, parental awareness and use of ESRB video game ratings has steadily increased through the years. The study involved more than 500 parents of children aged 3 to 17 who play video games. Of those parents surveyed, 83 percent said that they are aware of the ESRB ratings, and 74 percent use the ratings regularly when buying games for their families.

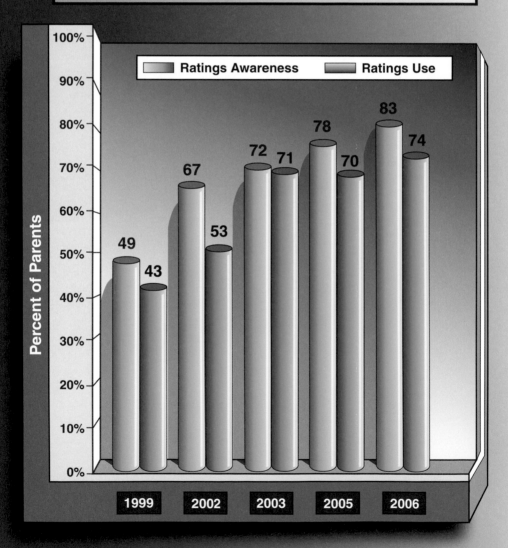

Source: Entertainment Software Rating Board, "Awareness, Use and Trust of ESRB Video Game Ratings Reach Historical High-Point Among Parents," March 29, 2006. www.esrb.org.

- According to a 2005 study by the Pew Research Center, **79 percent of the parents surveyed** said that when children are exposed to graphic violence or sex in entertainment, it is because of poor parental supervision rather than the result of inadequate laws.

- In the same Pew Research poll, **62 percent of parents surveyed** said there is enough information available to help them decide which video games are appropriate for their children, and most said they have a fair amount of trust in the current rating system.

- In an April 2007 survey by the FTC, **7 percent of parents** said that one of their under-17 children's favorite games is M-rated, while **23 percent of the children** surveyed said one of their favorite games is M-rated.

Key People and Advocacy Groups

Craig Anderson: Anderson is chair of the psychology department at Iowa State University and has written numerous publications about the connection between video games and aggression in children. Along with Douglas A. Gentile and Katherine E. Buckley, Anderson coauthored the book *Violent Video Game Effects on Children and Adolescents.*

Douglas A. Gentile: Gentile runs the Media Research Lab at Iowa State University and has done research on violent video games and aggression. Along with his father, J. Ronald Gentile, he coauthored a paper entitled "Violent Video Games as Exemplary Teachers: A Conceptual Analysis."

Henry Jenkins: Jenkins is a professor and director of comparative studies at the Massachusetts Institute of Technology, as well as an avid video game enthusiast. Jenkins has spoken and written extensively on the myths that convince people video games are harmful.

Gerard Jones: Jones is a comic-book writer and screenwriter, as well as the author of *Killing Monsters: Why Children NEED Fantasy, Super Heroes, and Make-Believe Violence.* He is well-known for his stance on violent video games, saying that they provide children with a fantasy world in which they learn to control their emotions of anger and violence.

Douglas Lowenstein: Lowenstein founded the Entertainment Software Association and served as its president until 2007. He now heads an industry trade organization called The Private Equity Council.

Dennis McCauley: McCauley is an outspoken critic of video game legislation and a staunch supporter of the video game industry remaining self-regulated. He writes and maintains a Web site called GamePolitics. com whose tagline is "Where politics and video games collide."

Jack Thompson: Thompson is a well-known Florida attorney who is one of the most outspoken critics of violent video games. He has argued for acquittal of defendants in violent crime cases in which he was convinced the games were responsible for the crimes. Thompson is also known for attempting to ban certain types of music and trying to have Howard Stern's show removed from an Orlando, Florida, radio station.

Patricia Vance: Vance, the current president of the ESRB, is responsible for overseeing and enforcing the computer and video game industry's self-regulatory practices.

Daphne White: White is executive director of The Lion & Lamb Project, which is a national grassroots organization whose goal is to stop the marketing of violent entertainment to children.

Elizabeth (Liz) Woolley: After her son, Shawn, became addicted to the video game *EverQuest* and shot himself to death in November 2001, Woolley formed Online Gamers Anonymous.

Chronology

1962
MIT graduate student and programmer Steve "Slug" Russell releases *Spacewar*, the first interactive computer game.

1980
Japanese amusement company Namco Limited releases *Pac-Man*, the most popular arcade game of all time, and licenses Midway Games to sell it in the United States.

1971
Computer engineer Nolan Bushnell creates an arcade version of *Spacewar* called *Computer Space*, which is designed to be used with a standard television set.

1979
Milton Bradley releases Microvision, the first handheld programmable game system.

1960   1965   1970   1975   1980

1968
Engineer Ralph Baer develops Brown Box (including a target shooting "rifle"), the first game system designed to be attached to a normal television set.

1976
Exidy Games releases a crude arcade game called *Death Race*, in which players drive over stick men that scream and squeal and are replaced on-screen by tombstones. The game becomes a subject of controversy and is featured on the CBS program *60 Minutes*.

1981
Arcade revenues in the United States reach $5 billion.

1972
Using Baer's Brown Box technology, Magnavox launches the Odyssey game console, the world's first home video game system. Atari engineer Al Alcorn creates an arcade game called *Pong* and installs the first coin-operated *Pong* machine in a Sunnyvale, California, bar called Andy Capp's Tavern. The game becomes a huge success.

1982
Video game sales in the United States gross more than $3 billion per year.

1986
Nintendo releases the Nintendo Entertainment System (NES), Sega releases the Sega Master System, and Atari releases the 7800 game console. As home video game systems become more popular, arcades throughout the United States suffer.

1993
Game developers Ed Boon and John Tobias release the home version of their game *Mortal Kombat*, which creates public concern because of its graphic, realistic violence.

2005
Senators Hillary Clinton and Joseph Lieberman are unsuccessful at passing national legislation known as the Family Entertainment Protection Act to help keep M-rated video games out of the hands of children.

2001
Video game sales in the United States reach $6.1 billion.

1985   1990   1995   2000   2005

1989
Nintendo releases its Game Boy, a handheld video game console that is bundled with the puzzle game *Tetris*.

1994
The Interactive Digital Software Association (later renamed the Entertainment Software Association) is formed as the interactive entertainment industry's trade and lobbying association. The Entertainment Software Rating Board is formed as an independent video game rating organization.

1997
Hundreds of children in Japan suffer seizures while watching a cartoon program based on *Pokémon*. Researchers discover that flashing colored lights on the screen can trigger photosensitive epilepsy.

2006
Video game sales in the United States reach $7.4 billion.

2007
The ESRB announces its commitment to ongoing education of 10,000 retailers with regard to enforcing video game ratings.

1996
Nintendo releases the video game *Pokémon* for its Game Boy system in Japan, and it skyrockets in popularity.

Related Organizations

Academy of Interactive Arts & Sciences (AIAS)

23622 Calabasas Rd., Suite 220

Calabasas, CA 91302

phone: (818) 876-0826 • fax: (818) 876-0850

e-mail: info@interactive.org • Web site: www.interactive.org

The AIAS is a nonprofit organization that promotes entertainment software such as video and computer games. It publishes interviews, stories, and news on its Web site and holds an Interactive Achievement Award ceremony each year.

Common Sense Media

1550 Bryant St., Suite 555

San Francisco, CA 94103

phone: (415) 863-0600 • fax: (415) 863-0601

e-mail: info@commonsensemedia.org

Web site: www.commonsensemedia.org

Common Sense Media is a nonpartisan, nonprofit organization whose goal is to provide trustworthy information on media and entertainment content to the public. Its Web site includes research reports, video game reviews and advisories, current news, tips for parents, and a monthly newsletter.

Entertainment and Leisure Software Publishers Association (ELSPA)

167 Wardour St.

London, United Kingdom W1F 8WL

phone: +44 20 7534 0580 • fax:+44 20 7534 0581

e-mail: info@elspa.com • Web site: www.elspa.com

Formerly known as the European Leisure Software Publishers Association, the ELSPA works to protect, promote, and provide for the interests of its members, while addressing issues that affect the computer and video game industries. The organization provides sales data for games sold in the United Kingdom and promotes antipiracy initiatives. It also comanages the London Games Festival and the Edinburgh Interactive Festival.

Entertainment Consumers Association (ECA)

64 Danbury Rd., Suite 700

Wilton, CT 06897-4406

phone: (203) 761-6180 • fax: (203) 761-6184

e-mail: feedback@theeca.com • Web site: www.theeca.com

The ECA is an advocacy group that works on behalf of people who play computer and video games, and is against any sort of antigame legislation. The group publishes a blog titled GamePolitics.com, which features politically oriented news and opinions about video games, the video game business, and the role video games play in modern society.

Entertainment Merchants Association (EMA)

16530 Ventura Blvd., Suite 400

Encino, CA 91436-4551

phone: (818) 385-1500 • fax: (818) 385-0567

e-mail: emaoffice@entmerch.org • Web site: www.entmerch.org

The EMA is dedicated to advancing the interests of the $33 billion home entertainment industry. EMA represents approximately 600 companies throughout the United States, Canada, and other countries.

Entertainment Software Association (ESA)

575 Seventh St. NW, Suite 300

Washington, DC 20004

phone: (202) 223-2400 • fax: (202) 223-2401

e-mail: esa@theesa.com • Web site: www.theesa.com

The ESA is the trade association of the computer and video game industry in the United States. Its Web site provides facts, articles, and research. One of the ESA's projects is the Video Game Voters Network (www.video gamevoters.org), a grassroots political network for video game enthusiasts.

Entertainment Software Rating Board (ESRB)

317 Madison Ave., 22nd Fl.

New York, NY 10017

phone: (212) 759-0700

e-mail: info@esrb.org • Web site: www.esrb.org

The ESRB is a self-regulatory organization that applies and enforces ratings, advertising guidelines, and online privacy principles for video and computer games and other entertainment software in the United States and Canada.

International Game Developers Association (IGDA)

19 Mantua Rd.

Mt. Royal, NJ 08061

phone: (856) 423-2990 • fax: (856)-423-3420

e-mail: contact@igda.org • Web site: www.igda.org

IGDA is a professional society for video and computer game developers throughout the world.

National Institute on Media and the Family

606 24th Ave. S., Suite 606

Minneapolis, MN 55454

phone: (612) 672-5437 • toll-free: (888) 672-5437

fax: (612) 672-4113

e-mail: info@mediafamily.org • Web site: www.mediafamily.org

The National Institute on Media and the Family is a research-based organization that focuses on the positive and negative effects of media on children and youth. It publishes fact sheets, an e-newsletter called *Media-Wise*, columns, and other educational information.

Online Gamers Anonymous

PO Box 5646

Harrisburg, PA 17110

phone: (612) 245-1115

e-mail: olga@olganon.org • Web site: www.olganonboard.org

Online Gamers Anonymous is a self-help organization that is dedicated to helping people who are addicted to video games, as well as their families. The Web site offers "twelve-step" guidance for addicts, daily readings, online chats, and message boards.

Parents Television Council (PTC)

707 Wilshire Blvd. #2,075

Los Angeles, CA 90017

phone: (213) 403-1300 • toll-free: (800) 882-6868

fax: (213) 403-1301

e-mail: editor@parentstv.org • Web site: www.parentstv.org

The PTC is a nonpartisan organization that works with government officials, as well as representatives of the entertainment industry, to ensure that what is shown on television or appears in video games is not harmful to children. Its Web site offers game reviews, information about legislative efforts, news releases, and publications.

For Further Research

Books

Craig A. Anderson, Douglas A. Gentile, and Katherine E. Buckley, *Violent Video Game Effects on Children and Adolescents.* New York: Oxford University Press, 2007.

John C. Beck and Mitchell Wade, *Got Game: How the Gamer Generation Is Reshaping Business Forever.* Boston: Harvard Business School Press, 2004.

Brenda Brathwaite, *Sex in Video Games.* Boston: Charles River Media, 2007.

Edward Castronova, *Synthetic Worlds: The Business and Culture of Online Games.* Chicago: University of Chicago Press, 2005.

James Paul Gee, *What Video Games Have to Teach Us About Learning and Literacy.* New York: Palgrave Macmillan, 2003.

Mark D. Griffiths, *Gambling and Gaming Addictions in Adolescence.* Malden, MA: British Psychological Society, 2002.

David Haugen and Susan Musser, eds., *At Issue: Video Games.* Detroit: Greenhaven, 2007.

Steven Johnson, *Everything Bad Is Good for You.* New York: Riverhead, 2005.

Jesper Juul, *Half-Real: Video Games Between Real Rules and Fictional Worlds.* Cambridge, MA: MIT Press, 2005.

Bill Maier, *Help! My Child Is Hooked on Video Games.* Carol Stream, IL: Tyndale House, 2006.

Marc Prensky, *Don't Bother Me Mom—I'm Learning!* St. Paul, MN: Paragon House, 2006.

David Williamson Shaffer, *How Computer Games Help Children Learn.* New York: Palgrave Macmillan, 2007.

Karen Sternheimer, *It's Not the Media: The Truth About Pop Culture's Influence on Children.* Boulder, CO: Westview, 2003.

Jack Thompson, *Out of Harm's Way*. Wheaton, IL: Tyndale House, 2005.

Mark J.P. Wolf and Bernard Perron, *The Video Game Theory Reader*. New York, London: Routledge, 2003.

Periodicals

Jane Avrich, Steven Johnson, Raph Koster, Tomas de Zengotita, and Bill Wasik, "Grand Theft Education: Literacy in the Age of Video Games," *Harper's*, September 2006.

Jami Barenthin and Marieke van Puymbroeck, "Research Update—the Joystick Generation: Video Games Have Measurable Social Effects on Adolescents," *Parks & Recreation*, August 2006.

Paul Ryan Hiebert, "Games for People Who Want to Change the World," *Canadian Dimension*, November/December 2006.

Mary Jane Irwin, "Rated V for Violence: Legislation Against Video Games Is Ramping Up," *PC Magazine*, March 7, 2006.

Ben Kelly, "Law on Violent Video Games Languishes in Limbo," *West Covina (CA) San Gabriel Valley Tribune*, January 11, 2006.

David Kushner, "Off Target," *Electronic Gaming Monthly*, August 1, 2007.

Brian Lowry, "TV Watches as Games Take Heat," *Variety*, October 17, 2005.

Marie Price, "Federal Judge Strikes Down Okla.'s Violent Video Game Law," *Oklahoma City Journal Record*, September 18, 2007.

Robert D. Richards and Clay Calvert, "Target Real Violence, Not Video Games," *Christian Science Monitor*, August 1, 2005.

Daniel Ruth, "It's Not Called 'Grand Theft' for Nothing!" *Tampa (FL) Tribune*, July 29, 2005.

Greg Sandoval, "Do Video Games Need a Woman's Touch?" *Buffalo (NY) News*, August 8, 2005.

Allie Shah and Patrice Relerford, "A Story of Sex, Lies and Video Games: 'San Andreas' Sparks Latest Fracas in Battle over Cultural Boundaries," *Minneapolis Star Tribune*, July 23, 2005.

Mike Snider, "Violence in the Docket," *USA Today*, October 6, 2005.

Janine Wood, "Why Moms Give In to Video Games," *Christian Science Monitor*, May 4, 2007.

Internet Sources

John Berman, "Do Video Games Make Kids Smarter?" ABC News, June 2, 2005. http://abcnews.go.com/WNT/Health/story?id=814080& page=1.

Candace Lombardi, "Are Violent Video Games Really a Problem?" CNET News, August 2, 2006. www.news.com/2100-1043_3-6101471.html.

Andrea Lynn, "No Strong Link Seen Between Violent Video Games and Aggression," News Bureau, University of Illinois at Urbana-Champaign, August 9, 2005. www.news.uiuc.edu/news/05/0809videogames.html.

Michigan State University, "Violent Video Games Lead to Brain Activity Characteristic of Aggression," news release, October 12, 2005. http://newsroom.msu.edu/site/indexer/2532/content.htm.

NYU Child Study Center, "Video Games: Cons and Pros." www. aboutour kids. org/aboutour/articles/video_games.html.

Carolyn Sayre, "Video Games That Keep Kids Fit," *Time.com*, September 12, 2007. www.time.com/time/magazine/article/0,9171,1661688,00. html.

Deborah Sherman, "More Videogames, Fewer Books at Schools?" Reuters, March 16, 2007. http://uk.reuters.com/article/technologyNews/idUKN1642567920070316.

60 Minutes, CBSNews, "Can a Video Game Lead to Murder?" March 6, 2005. www.cbsnews.com/stories/2005/03/04/60minutes/main6782 61.shtml.

Brad Zambrello, "Video Game Addiction Harmful," *Daily Campus*, September 20, 2005. www.dailycampus.com/media/storage/paper3 40/news/2005/09/20/Commentary/Video.Game.Addiction.Harm ful-991128.shtml.

Source Notes

Overview

1. Steven L. Kent, *The Ultimate History of Video Games.* Roseville, CA: Prima, 2001, p. 19.
2. Henry Jenkins, "Reality Bytes: Eight Myths About Video Games Debunked," *The Video Game Revolution*, PBS, December 2004. www.pbs.org.
3. Christopher Bantick, "Why Computer Games Should Worry Parents," *Age*, January 15, 2004. www.theage.com.au.
4. Media Awareness Network, "Special Issues for Young Children." www.media-awareness.ca.
5. Quoted in Wanda Beneditti, "Were Video Games to Blame for Massacre?" MSNBC, April 20, 2007. www.msnbc.msn.com.
6. Robert D. Richards and Clay Calvert, "Target Real Violence, Not Video Games," *Christian Science Monitor*, August 1, 2005. www.csmonitor.com.
7. Quoted in SixWise.com, "TV and Video Gaming During Weekdays Does Harm Student Performance," October 11, 2006. www.sixwise.com.
8. Quoted in Jim Casey, "Excerpts from C.S. Lewis, *The Screwtape Letters*," University of Alabama, April 19, 2005. http://bama.ua.edu.
9. David Walsh, Douglas Gentile, Erin Walsh, and Nat Bennett, "Eleventh Annual MediaWise®Video Game Report Card," National Institute on Media and the Family, November 28, 2006. www.mediafamily.org.
10. Quoted in Bruce Japsen and Eric Benderoff, "AMA May Identify Excessive Video Game Play as Addiction," *Los Angeles Times*, June 25, 2007. www.latimes.com.
11. Quoted in Valerie Wencis, "Most Middle School Boys and Many Girls Play Violent Video Games," news release, Massachusetts General Hospital, June 29, 2007. www.mgh.harvard.edu.
12. Quoted in Carrie Kilman, "Video Games: Playing Against Racism,"Tolerance.org, June 8, 2005. www.tolerance.org.
13. Aleah Tierney, "What Women Want," *The Video Game Revolution*, PBS, September 2004. www.pbs.org.
14. Quoted in Entertainment Software Association, "Essential Facts About the Computer and Video Game Industry," May 10, 2006. www.theesa.com.

Are Video Games Harmful?

15. Bantick, "Why Computer Games Should Worry Parents."
16. Quoted in Stanley A. Miller, "Death of a Game Addict," *Milwaukee Journal Sentinel*, March 31, 2002. www.jsonline.com/story/index.aspx?id=31536.
17. Sonya S. Brady and Karen A. Matthews, "Effects of Media Violence on Health-Related Outcomes Among Young Men," *Archives of Pediatrics & Adolescent Medicine*, April 2006. http://archpedi.ama-assn.org.
18. Jenkins, "Reality Bytes."
19. Quoted in Tim Surette, "NFS Found in Fatal Drag-Racing Car Crash," GameSpot.com, January 26, 2006. www.gamespot.com.
20. Quoted in NYU Child Study Center, "Video Games: Cons and Pros." www.aboutourkids.org.

21. Steve Pritchard, interview with the author, November 7, 2007.

22. Pritchard, interview.

23. Quoted in Amazon.com, "New Super Mario Bros.: Product Features." www.amazon.com.

24. Lee Wilson, "Getting It Wrong: Slaying Myths About Video Games (Part 2)," TechLearning, October 15, 2007. www.techlearning.com.

25. Quoted in David Williamson Shaffer, *How Computer Games Help Children Learn.* New York: Palgrave MacMillan, 2006, p. x.

Do Video Games Cause Violent Crime?

26. Quoted in *60 Minutes*, CBS News, "Can a Video Game Lead to Murder?" June 17, 2005. www.cbsnews.com.

27. Jonathan M. Gitlin, "New Survey Shows That Kids Like Games Rated M for Mature," Ars Technica, July 3, 2007. http://arstechnica.com.

28. Quoted in *Executive Intelligence Review*, "The Research Is In: Violent Video Games Can Lead to Violent Behavior," June 1, 2007. www.larouchepub.com.

29. Craig A. Anderson, "Violent Video Games: Myths, Facts, and Unanswered Questions," *Psychological Science Agenda*, American Psychological Association, October 2003. www.apa.org.

30. Tyler Staples, interview with the author, November 8, 2007.

31. Quoted in Tracy McVeigh, "Computer Games Stunt Teen Brains," *Guardian Unlimited*, August 19, 2001. http://observer.guardian.co.uk.

32. Quoted in Kristin Kaining, "Does Game Violence Make Teens Aggressive?" MSNBC.com, December 8, 2006. www.msnbc.msn.com.

33. Quoted in Candace Lombardi, "Are Violent Video Games Really a Problem?" *Technology News*, ZDNet, August 2, 2006. http://news.zdnet.com.

34. Quoted in Siobhan Morrissey, "A Surge in Cop Killings, *Time*, September 28, 2007. www.time.com.

35. Quoted in Kristina Nwazota, "Judge Weighs Ban on Violent Video Game Sales," *NewsHour*, PBS, July 16, 2003. www.pbs.org.

36. Broadband, "Top 10 Most Violent Video Games," DX Gaming, April 2, 2007. www.dxgaming.com.

How Do Video Games Affect Mental and Physical Health?

37. Quoted in Mariella Savidge, "Do Video Games Harm Young Boys?" *Morning Call*, March 20, 2006. www.mcall.com.

38. Quoted in BBC News, "Computer Game Teenager Gets DVT," January 29, 2004. http://news.bbc.co.uk.

39. Chris Morris, "This Is Science? Excessive Gaming Can Make Kids Fat. In Other News, So Can Doughnuts," CNNMoney.com, July 6, 2004. http://money.cnn.com.

40. Quoted in Anthony Faiola, "When Escape Seems Just a Mouse-Click Away," *Washington Post*, May 27, 2006, p. A-1.

41. Quoted in Faiola, "When Escape Seems Just a Mouse-Click Away."

42. Nintendo, "Health & Safety Precautions for Cartridge-Based Consoles." www.nintendo.com.

43. Betsy Streisand, "Not Just Child's Play," *U.S. News & World Report*, August 6, 2006. http://health.usnews.com.

44. Quoted in Christopher Lee, "Video Games Aim to Hook Children on Better Health," *Washington Post*, October 21, 2006. www.washingtonpost.com.

45. Jeff Gerstmann, "Dance Dance Revolution Extreme," GameSpot, September 21, 2004. www.gamespot.com.
46. Quoted in Allison Barker, "Study Uses Video Games to Fight Obesity, *USA Today*, April 2, 2005. www.usatoday.com.
47. Quoted in Robert Wood Johnson Foundation, "$8.25-Million Research Program to Investigate Design Strategies and Benefits of Interactive Games to Improve Health and Health Care," November 12, 2007. www.rwjf.org.

Should Video Games Be Regulated?

48. Kent, *The Ultimate History of Video Games*, p. 464.
49. Quoted in Joint Hearings Before the Subcommittee on Juvenile Justice, 103rd Congress, Serial No. J-103-37, December 9, 1993, March 4 and July 29, 1994, p. 20.
50. Quoted in Entertainment Software Rating Board, "Senators Hillary Rodham Clinton and Joe Lieberman Join ESRB to Launch Nationwide Video Game Ratings TV PSA Campaign," December 7, 2006. www.esrb.org.
51. Common Sense Media, "Violent Video Games and Our Kids," 2005. www.commonsensemedia.org.
52. Quoted in Alexa Smith, "Faith Groups Go After Violent Video Game Marketing," *Presbyterian News Service*, January 19, 2005. www.pcusa.org.
53. Walsh, Gentile, Walsh, and Bennett, "Eleventh Annual MediaWise® Video Game Report Card."
54. Adam D. Thierer, "Regulating Video Games: Parents or Uncle Sam?" Cato Institute, July 14, 2003. www.cato.org.
55. David Grossman, "Teaching Kids to Kill," *Phi Kappa Phi National Forum*, Fall 2000. www.killology.com.

List of Illustrations

Are Video Games Harmful?
Who Plays Video Games?   33
Top-Selling Video Games in 2006   34
Youth Video Game Addiction   35

Do Video Games Cause Violent Crime?
Juvenile Crime Rises with Video Game Sales (2000–2006)   48
Mature (M)-Rated Video Game Sales to Children Decreasing   49
Which Video Games Are Most Violent?   50

How Do Video Games Affect Mental and Physical Health?
Video Game Usage and Childhood Obesity Rising   65
Video Games and Physical Ailments   66
How Violent Video Games Affect the Brain   67

Should Video Games Be Regulated?
Video Game Legislation   81
Americans' View of Government Video Game Regulation   82
What Do Video Game Ratings Mean to Parents?   84

List of Illustrations

Index

addiction, to video games, 9, 29
  experience in South Korea, 54–55, 64
  prevalence of, 35
  suicide and, 22–23
  symptoms of, 17–18
Age of Mythology (video game), 17
American Academy of Child & Adolescent
  Psychiatry (AACAP), 51
American Academy of Pediatrics (AAP), 43
American Medical Association (AMA), 18
American Society of Hand Therapists, 52
Anderson, Craig, 21, 37–38
Archives of Pediatrics & Adolescent Medicine
  (journal), 24

Baca, Joe, 30
Bantick, Christopher, 13, 22, 29
Beck, John C., 29
Bennett, Nat, 28
Better Health Channel, 62
Biggs, John, 30
Blagojevich, Rod, 78
Brady, Sonya S., 23, 24
brain
  effects of violent video games on, 67
    (illustration)
  video games associated with changes in,
    39–40
Brody, Peter, 61
Brouse, Jack, 71–72

Calvert, Clay, 14, 28, 43
Cantor, Joanne, 31
Carll, Elizabeth, 44
Chase, Robert, 69
children. *See* juveniles
Cho Seung-Hui, 14
Clinton, Hillary Rodham, 30, 74
Cole, Steve, 57
Common Sense Media, 79
computers, sales growth in, 65 (chart)
Cooper, Charles, 76
crimes
  juvenile
    correlation with video game sales, 48
    (chart)

    trends in, 48
  violent
    active nature of video games and, 37–38
    association with video game playing,
      9, 14
      conflicting positions on, 43, 44, 46
    increase in violent video game playing
      and, 40–42
    trends in, 47
Crump, James, 36
Cumberbatch, Guy, 30

Dance Dance Revolution (video game), 58, 67
deep vein thrombosis (DVT), 52–53
Della Rocca, Jason, 41
Dickerson, Mary Lou, 78
Duke Nukem (video game), 14

Entertainment Software Association (ESA),
  11, 72
  on characteristics of video game players,
    32, 33 (chart)
  founding of, 80
  opposition to video game regulation,
    73–74
  on top-selling video games, 34 (table)
Entertainment Software Rating Board
  (ESRB), 8, 12
  formation of, 80
Epilepsy Foundation, 55, 64
Escape from Diab (video game), 17
ESRB. *See* Entertainment Software Rating
  Board
ESRB Retail Council, 72

Family Entertainment Protection Act
  (proposed, 2005), 74
Farrell, Patricia A., 60
Federal Bureau of Investigation (FBI), 41
Federal Trade Commission (FTC), 47, 49,
  70, 80
Ferris, Duke, 45
First Amendment, video games protected by,
  9, 73–74, 79
Fisher, Ken, 77
Fitcheard, Larry, 19

fitness games (exergames), 58
Forbes (magazine), 33

Gallagher, Richard, 25
gamers
    average age of, 11
    characteristics of, 32, 33 (chart)
Gears of War (video game), 26, 33, 34, 50
Gee, James Paul, 13, 17, 27, 62
Gentile, Douglas, 28
Gerstmann, Jeff, 58
Gitlin, Jonathan M., 37
Gitlow, Stuart, 18
God of War (video game), 14, 50
Gonzalez, Brian O., 36
Grand Theft Auto (video game), 11, 24, 34,
    34, 37, 38, 42, 50
Grossman, David, 41, 45, 74

Hahn, Jeremy, 57
Haninger, Kevin, 47, 71
health effects, of video game playing, 9, 17
    overweight/obesity among youth, 53–54
        conflicting views on, 62
    photosensitive epilepsy, 55–56, 64
    physical ailments, 52–53, 66 (illustration)
Health Games Research program (Robert
    Wood Johnson Foundation), 58–59
Hill, Jason, 51

Igniq, 77

Jenkins, Henry, 12, 24, 46
Johnson, Steven, 61
Journal of the American Medical Association, 71
juveniles
    availability of M-rated games to, 47
    benefits of video games to, 12–13, 27
    crimes by
        correlation with video game sales, 48
            (chart)
        trends in, 48
    increase in time spent playing M-rated
        games by, 33
    prevalence of overweight/obesity among,
        64, 65 (chart)
    risks of video games to, 13–14
    video game hours per week, by age group/
        gender, 35 (chart)
    video game playing and overweight/obesity

among, 53–54

Kaiser Family Foundation, 13, 35
Kawashima, Ryuta, 39–40
Keigwin, Adam, 68
Kent, Steven L., 10–11, 69
Kim Myung, 54–55

Lambert, Robrietta, 58
Lavelle, Peter, 61
Lewis, C.S., 17
Lieberman, Joseph, 69, 74
Lightwood, Marcie, 44
Lobsinger, Paul, 25
Lowenstein, Douglas, 20, 31, 76

Madden NFL '07 (video game), 26, 34
Marketing Violent Entertainment to Children
    (Federal Trade Commission), 49, 70
Mathews, Vincent P., 67
Matrix Reloaded (video game), 42
Matthews, Karen A., 23, 24
Mayo Clinic, 62
McPherson, Terence, 44
Media Awareness Network, 14
Moore, Devin, 36–37
Morris, Chris, 53
Mortal Kombat (video game), 14, 50, 68–69,
    80

Nanoswarm: Invasion from Inner Space (video
    game), 17
National Institute on Media and the Family,
    11, 15, 23
    on children's game playing and overweight/
        obesity, 64
    on children's *vs.* parents' perceptions of
        parental involvement, 73
    on heaviest video game players, 32
    on symptoms of video game addiction,
        17–18
    on time spent on video games and grades,
        15
National Institutes of Health (NIH), 17
Newitz, Annalee, 44
New Super Mario Bros. (video game), 26, 34

Olson, Cheryl K., 19
Ontiveros, Sue, 78
Onyekere, Chinwe, 59

Pakeerah, Giselle, 78
parents
    awareness/use of ratings by, 72–73, 84
        (chart)
    percentage having any rules for video game
        use, 35 (chart)
    surveys of, 85
Parents Television Council (PTC), 46
Parker, Jay, 23
Patino, Monzerratt, 57
Patrick, Dominic, 52–53
Pew Research Center, 85
photosensitive epilepsy, 55–56
Pierce, Karen, 61
Playing Video Games (British Board of Film
    Classification), 47
Pokéman (video game), 55
Pritchard, Steve, 25–26

Radford, Benjamin, 29
ratings, ESRB
    assignment of, 69–70
    effectiveness of, 70–71
    parents' attitudes on, 85
    parents' awareness/use of, 84 (chart)
    retailers are not bound by, 71–72
regulation, 8
    attitudes on government role in, 82 (chart),
        83 (chart)
    conflicting positions on, 76–79
    debate over, 68–69
    First Amendment and, 9, 73–74, 79
    states' efforts at, 80, 81 (map)
    in U.S. *vs.* other countries, 12
Re-Mission (video game), 57
repetitive strain injury, 66
Richards, Robert D., 14, 28, 43
Robert Wood Johnson Foundation, 10, 58
Russell, Steve "Slug," 10

Sawyer, Ben, 62, 63
Schwarzenegger, Arnold, 77
Sharmat, Samuel, 60
S.M.A.R.T. BrainGames, 56
Smith, Paul M., 79
social skills, influence of video games on,
    18–19
Son Yeongi, 54
South Korea, video game addiction in,
    54–55, 64

Spacewar (video game), 10–11
Spio, Mary, 28
Staples, Tyler, 38–39
Streisand, Betsy, 56
Super Metroid (video game), 20

Taylor, Carol, 57
tendonitis, 52, 66
Thierer, Adam D., 68, 74, 79
Thompson, Jack, 14, 37
Thompson, Kimberly M., 47, 71
Tierney, Aleah, 19

The Ultimate History of Video Games (Kent),
    10–11, 69
United States
    spending on video games in, 8, 12, 32
    violent crime trends in, 41, 47

video games
    brain changes associated with, 39–40
    first, 10–11
    future of, 20
    growing popularity of, 8, 11
    may curb aggression, 42–43
    most popular types of, 26–27
    most violent, 50 (table)
    M-rated
        decline in sales to youth, 49 (chart), 72
        juvenile access to, 47
    negative racial/sexual stereotypes reinforced
        by, 19–20
    sales growth in, 65 (chart)
    therapeutic, 56–57, 64
    top-selling, 34 (table)
    T-rated, killing is rewarded/required in, 47
    See also gamers

Wade, Mitchell, 29
Walsh, David, 23, 28
Weingarten, Rebecca Kiki, 63
White, Daphne, 10
Whyte, Ronald, 21
Wilson, Lee, 27
Woolley, Liz, 22
Woolley, Shawn, 22
Wright, Will, 12

youth. *See* juveniles

About the Author

Peggy J. Parks holds a bachelor of science degree from Aquinas College in Grand Rapids, Michigan, where she graduated magna cum laude. She is a freelance author who has written more than 60 nonfiction educational books for children and young adults. Parks lives in Muskegon, Michigan, a town that she says inspires her writing because of its location on the shores of Lake Michigan.